FROM MALAGA TO PARIS
THE FORMATIVE YEARS OF
PABLO PICASSO

By Chris Wade

FROM MALAGA TO PARIS:
THE FORMATIVE YEARS OF PABLO PICASSO

Wisdom Twins Books, 2018
wisdomtwinsbooks.weebly.com

This edition released in 2018

Text Copyright of Chris Wade, 2018

FROM MALAGA TO PARIS
THE FORMATIVE YEARS OF
PABLO PICASSO

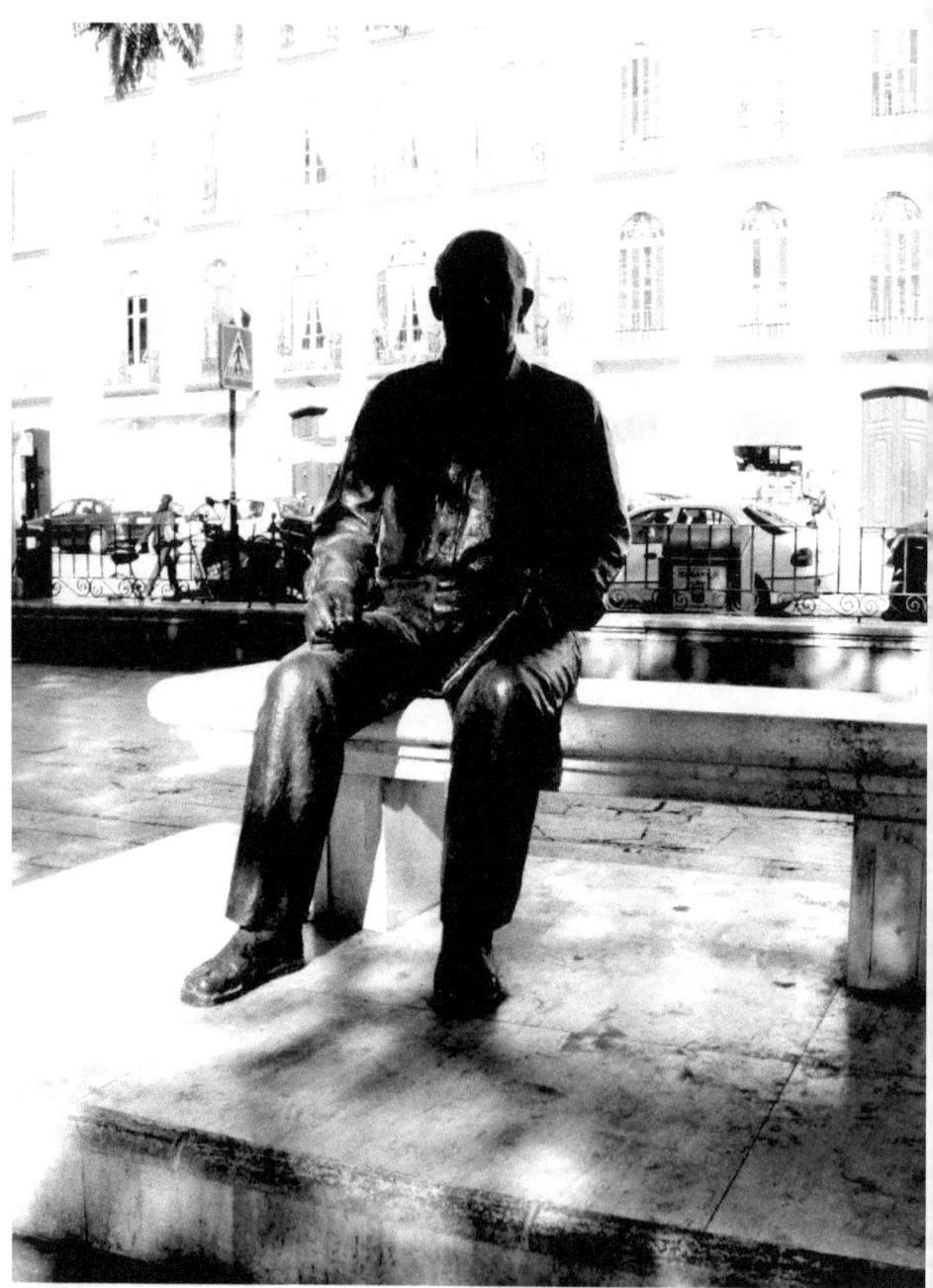

CONTENTS

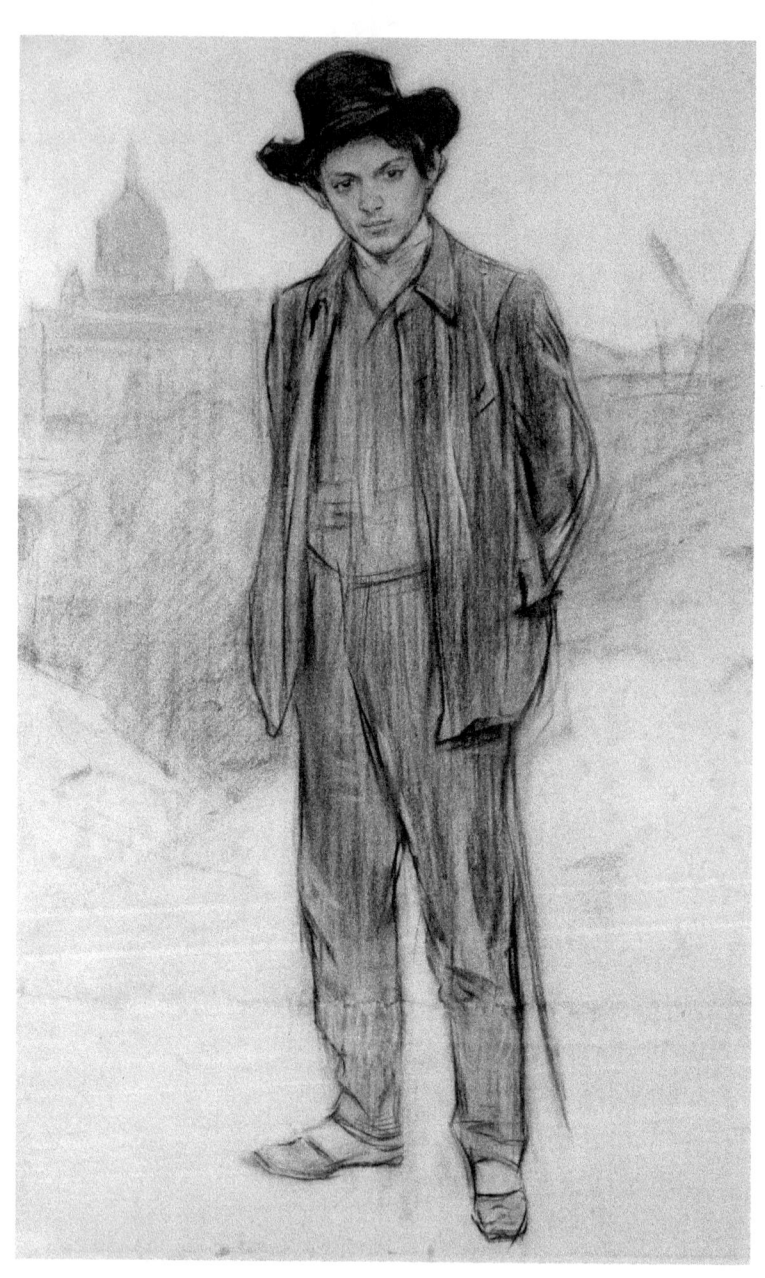

A portrait of Pablo Picasso by Ramon Casas, 1900

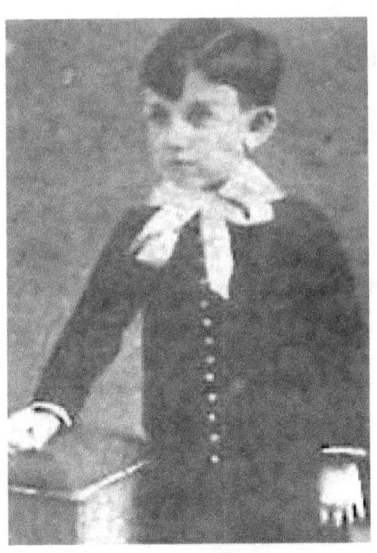

INTRODUCTION

"Every child is an artist. The problem is how to remain
an artist once we grow up."
- Picasso

It's forty five years since Pablo Picasso died, the artist who defined the 20th century in his paintings, drawings and sculptures. He was the first internationally famous artist who became a media hounded celebrity and remains perhaps the most iconic artist of all time. This is a man whose reputation is so large, so intimidating, so overpowering, that you often feel rather ridiculous attempting to define or assess his life and work at even the most vague level. As many true admirers know, for even those who dislike Picasso could not deny his influence, Picasso's life as an artist was long, winding, and epic in the truest sense. In many ways, it's still going on to this day, and it's a story unlikely to end for as long as people have an interest in the complexities of the human soul and wish to look at art in its most primal yet sophisticated form. Picasso studies are more impassioned than ever, as fans, critics and scholars dissect every era of his life for new clues about his genius. He seems to become more enigmatic yet relatable as the years go on.

One way to understand - or at least attempt to understand - many of the iconic Picasso traits, featured in both the man and his art, is to look at his roots. The early years, and by that I mean the 1800s until the turn of the 20th century, are often viewed as little more than an introduction into his life. For many, his true story took off in the 1900s when he began to redefine art on a personal level, when his work had repercussions and influence across the globe. But many of his mysteries and quirks can be traced back to his formative years, and most of them only truly make sense when exploring that time frame, before he became Picasso the icon. His life takes on a kind of domino knock on effect; when one act occurs, it triggers a new phase and a new era for his art and life, and this is true from the start.

His life began in the early 1880s, in Malaga, Southern Spain, as the son of a painter who wound up surpassing his academically skilled father, shunned formal training and found his feet in Paris. His works of the early 20th century, though largely uncelebrated at the time, have since become legendary, most notably those works done in what are known as the Blue and Rose periods, though these labels are sometimes viewed as rather lazy, considering the sheer breadth of both eras. He had already gained the trust and support of American art collector Gertrude Stein by 1905, and two years later he changed the rules with his spellbinding Les Demoiselles d'Avignon, which would remain one of the most important works of the 20th century. He invented styles and seemed to abandon them when they grew tiresome to him (Cubism for example, which he developed with Georges Braque from 1909 to 1912), learned to paint like a master before unravelling it all to access the purity of his inner child. It is the more colourful, broad and deceptively simplistic style which most people recognise as pure Picasso, but the iconic portraits of the 1930s onwards (including the more rushed and spirited later works, particularly those he did of his last wife Jacqueline) came about organically. Just like at the start, everything Picasso did didn't seem predetermined, but much of it was actually as a result of relentless, endlessly curious experimentation. He was the one holing himself up in dark studios to access the inner truth of what it is to be human.

Another useful and satisfying way to grasp his development is by taking a look through his gallery of self portraits, which in his early years fit perfectly in with his development and formative naivety. His first notable one came in 1896, when he was merely 15 years old. It's traditional, fittingly cracked due to age now, and resembles the work of countless artists of the era and much earlier. It harbours skill but seems suffocated with the kind of reserved academia his father Jose adored. Indeed, it's like the work of an old master, whereas Picasso was interested in becoming a new master.

His landmark 1899 led portrait is one of the most stunning, with Picasso catching his penetrating, almost ghostly glare in pencil. The self portraits advance with time, so it can be rewarding to view Picasso's self reflections while reading the time line of his life. They so often perfectly capture the mood of the times; for example, the Blue Period portrait of 1901 really does define that time, an era of hunger and desperation, but artistic stubbornness. His famous 1906 self-painting, though rather unlike the real Picasso of the time, reveals the more primitive influences which were creeping in by then. His 1907 self portrait, again, introduces a sizeable change, with more colour and some hasty jagged lines, those fish bowl eyes impossible to ignore. At the near end, his work remains up to date; like his 1965 self portrait, bearded and in a daze of stripes and child-like blurred perspective, which reflects the urgency and fear of his final chapter. His most haunting ones are the 1972 portraits, where he stares in fear, horror even, at the viewer. Picasso faced death full on just as he had faced life itself for almost a century. The self portraits offer the Picasso buff an alternative biography of penetrating stares and troubled eyes. They begin in the earliest days of his time as a serious artist, so one can compare the first self portraits with the final ones, picturing the monumental life that filled in the time between them.

We may choose to look at Picasso's work through the key works in the most important eras, and this too is a fine way to view the development of the artist. There are stand out works throughout, most prominently beginning in the so called Blue Period, with the likes of the Old Guitarist, that haunting portrait of the crooked backed homeless old man, and the disturbing portraits of his dead friend, Carles Cassagemas, whose suicide triggered off the grim ghostliness of the whole two year period.

The Rose period, of course, is more vibrant, with the harlequins and jugglers, while the portrait of his most famous patron, Gertrude Stein, also stands out as a landmark portrait. In his Cubist phase, nearly every surviving work reveals both the complexity and strange simplicity of this elongated experiment, particularly Girl with

Mandolin, while other, seemingly more trivial works like Bathers (1918) and Large Bather (1919) illustrate his dazzling range and lack of fear. Three Dancers, painted in 1925, remains one of his most iconic and unforgettable works, and his most famous flirtation with Surrealism. These are undeniably important works.

Other pictures reveal parts of Picasso's very soul. His bullfight paintings tell us much about Picasso's character and his fascination with this most supposedly noble of sports. His love of the game began, fittingly enough, in Malaga, the place he was born and lived until the age of 9. Again, the roots were in the childhood. The bullfight came out in other sections of his art too, as in the repeated presence of the Minotaur, the creature he often compared himself to, devouring and sacrificing women for the sake of his art. The matador, half man and half bull, is a figure that remains one of the most vital symbols in Picasso mythology.

Today, perhaps the two best known Picasso works are 1932's The Dream and 1937's politically charged and angry Guernica, two works which highlight the most important concerns of Pablo's life; his obsession with the mysteries of the female, and his need for world peace. Though his views and acts within these two fields of concerns were often paradoxical, Picasso's work seemed to make simple and approachable metaphors of both. His female portraits remain unmatched and while some of his political work has attracted criticism (his War and Peace mural for instance, as well as what people see as the lazy and overly simple emblems he created for peace), it is their simplicity and straight forwardness which keep them so vital and intimidating important today.

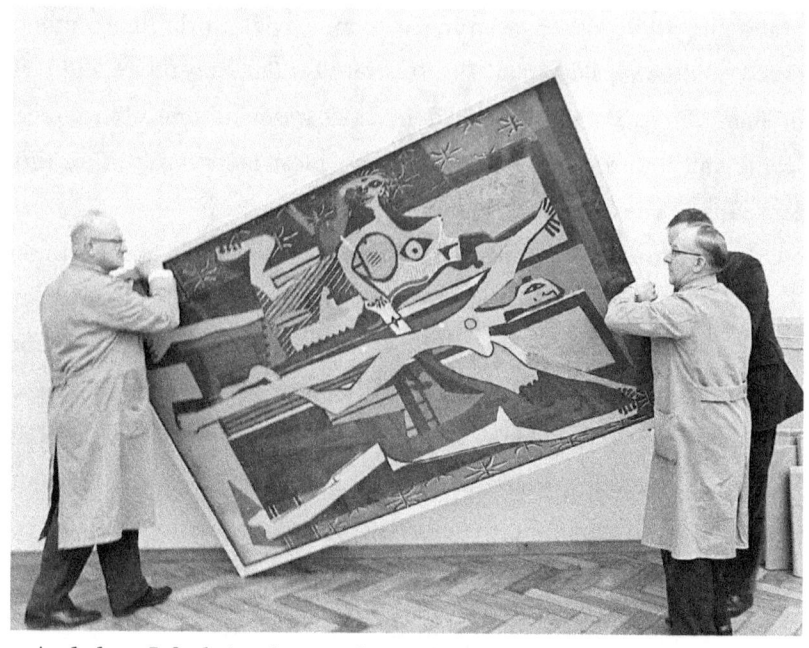

And that, I feel, is what explains the ever growing fascination and undying passion for Picasso's work. It defined the time but it remains timeless. While the work of other great artists of the 20th century may seem stuck in its era, Picasso's work seems to go on and on, transcending the ages. Though brilliant, much of the Surrealist works of the 1920s and 30s remain firmly in that period, at least in conceptual presentation, if not in attitude. (By the way, I myself remain a firm Surrealist.) However, the same cannot be said for Picasso's work, mainly because it was so personal, autobiographical, and open ended, so the viewer could invest their own ideas, views and personal feelings into the work. Whether you like all his work or not, it's fairly well understood that Picasso remains the most important and vital artist of the past hundred years, perhaps all time.

It is easy, especially these days, an era when Picasso's myth and personality match the interest in his work, to get lost in the legend of the man himself. It's also easy to judge and put down his work, dub it overrated or irrelevant. But these claims fall to the wayside when one stops and takes a serious look at the paintings, drawings, sketches, studies and sculptures; and not just his key works either, for a glimpse through his whole career (or as much as possible at least) reveals an unexpected gem at every turn. Sometimes the most unexpected works trigger off a reaction, an emotion, which makes them impenetrable enigmas. His work stays with you, and not just the pieces we are shown year after year and reminded of as vitally important in the evolution of modern art.

There are pockets of brilliance hidden in the time line; like the famous 1954 Sylvette paintings of the young Lydia Corbett, which are often overlooked these days. They get side stepped because they were not portraits of a mistress and therefore are dimmed in importance as being trivial, distractions even, from the personal anguish of his life at the time (his partner Francoise Gilot had just left him and he was yet to meet his last true love, Jacqueline Roque),; but the truth is they remain some of his most dazzling, positive, bright and wonderful works. Perhaps it's because they capture youth (she was 19 at the time), something the then 72 year old Picasso had not known for decades, since his early days in Paris. Again, it came back to the vitality of youth.

His latter day portraits of Jacqueline are similar, in which he has elevated her to a goddess like stature, yet these pure and marvellous works are rarely, if ever, judged against his taunting portraits of Dora Maar, his sexually powerful explorations into the mind of Marie-

Therese Walter, or his ever changing gallery of self portraits. What's so great about Picasso is that the works we are repeatedly shown are far from the full picture, and to some (me included) are anything but his best works. And some of them are hidden away in the first two decades of his life, so often skipped over and seen as little more than first stepping stones towards the great goal.

"He kept in his mind all those senses, all those images, all those smells and colours, which nourished and enriched his brain."
- Bernard Ruiz-Picasso on Pablo's childhood in Malaga

So you ask, why another book on Picasso? In early 2018 I wrote a small book on the artist's final three decades. My natural reaction, after examining his last chapters, was to look at the era that planted the roots of that remarkable life, his formative era, from his birth in 1881 to his breakthrough at the turn of the century, when he first went to Paris and returned, full of gloom, before entering his Blue Period. After this, there was no turning back. In these essays, I chart his rise from birth to his early time in Paris. All the eras, changes and shifts that followed were as a result of his earliest years, in Malaga, Barcelona, Madrid, and the first days in Paris. It all begins and forms in this time, and it's a vital period in understanding the man and the artist; his love of the bullfight; the paradoxical worship of his father and loathing of academia; his hatred of authority; his passion for drawing and so on. In the end, Picasso excelled at the one skill he had, and had become a compulsive creator who thought he could cheat death by constantly working, drawing, sculpting and painting.

As a young man, hustling his work in Paris, visiting sleazy brothels and chatting in cafes with other dreamers, would he have imagined such a rich, long and fruitful artistic life ahead of him? The answer might just be yes.

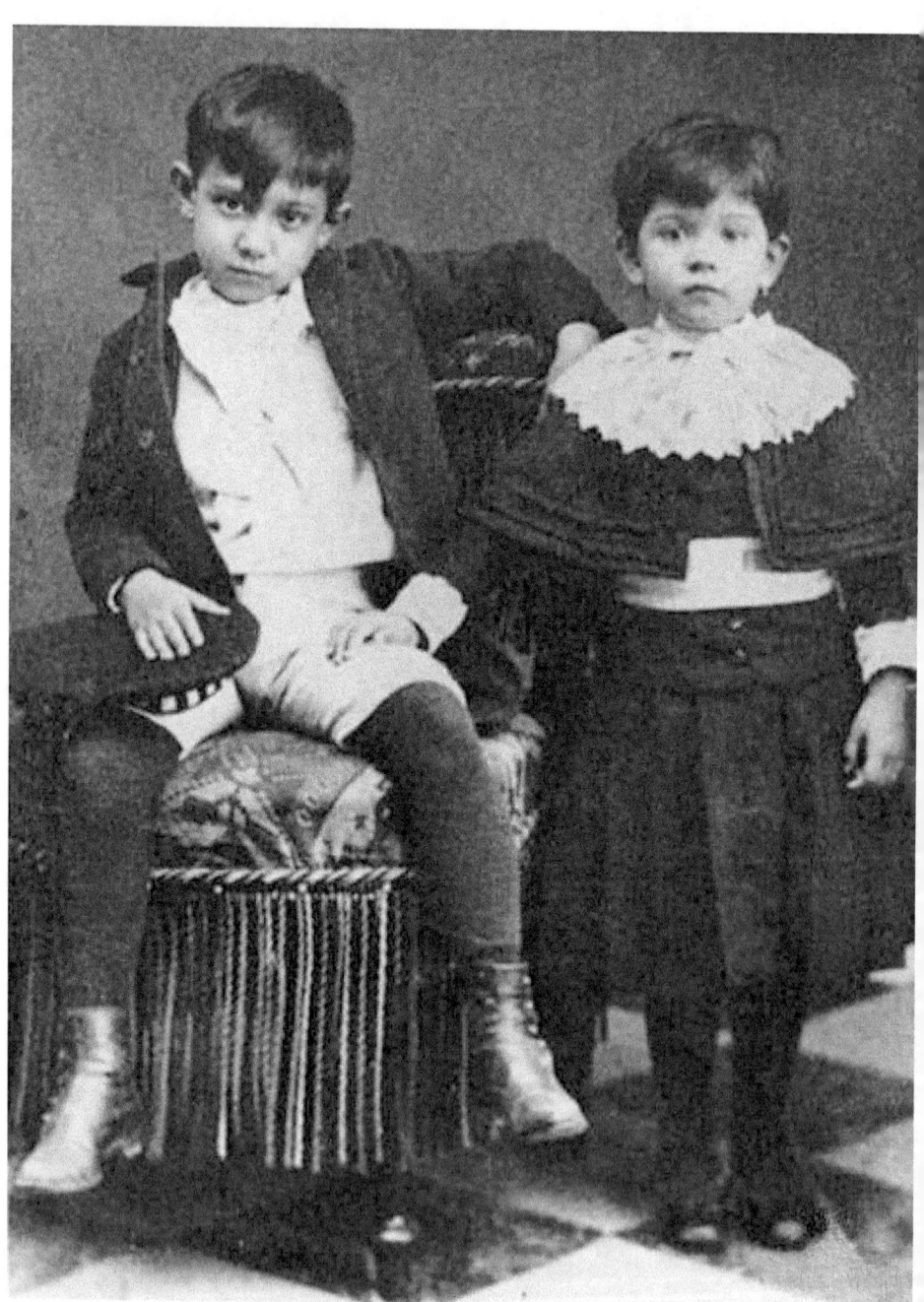

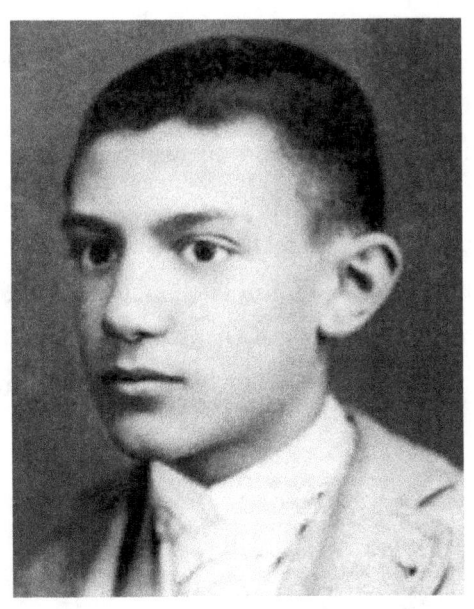

"WITH A GRIMACE AND A BELLOW OF FURY"

Picasso's Birth and Life in Malaga

"His mother was gaga about him."

- Claude Picasso

The city of Malaga, the birthplace of Pablo Picasso, still harbours the spirit of its most legendary son. Around every corner, the Picasso buff comes across one bit of Picasso related folk lore after another. The second largest city in Andalusia in Southern Spain, it's a place of wonder, equally striking and worn, both luxurious and earthy, contradictorily extravagant and plain. On one side of the city you have the bullring, which Picasso frequented as a boy, the Gibralfaro Castle on the hill which overlooks the whole of Malaga; then there are the ruins of the Roman theatre, where Picasso hung with the gypsies who taught him tricks, the river running through the centre, and the beautiful Malaga Cathedral, which remains one of the most popular tourist destinations of the city.

One of the other highly frequented hot spots is the building where Pablo was born, now a museum in his honour at Plaza de la Merced. He was born there on the 25th of October 1881, to his mother Maria Picasso y Lopez, and Don Jose Ruiz y Blasco, a painter and art teacher.

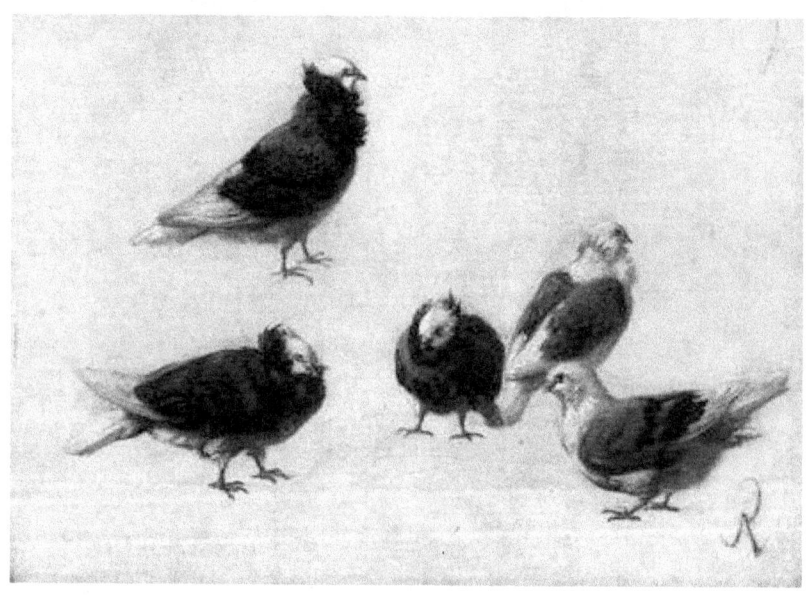

A painting by Picasso's father, Jose Ruiz y Blasco,
of his favourite subject, birds.

Some of the early stories of Picasso's life have entered the realm of unreal myth, and though they are irresistible and fitting with the legend's life to follow, they are also questionable. It is certain however that he was born dead and took a minute or so before calling out for the first time, as if he needed to consider whether this world was really for him. When the midwife had tried to revive his lifeless body on the table, she gave in and turned to the mother and father, ready to deliver the bad news. However, Don Salvador, Jose's younger brother, was thankfully present. Acting on impulse in the moment, he leant down and blew cigar smoke in baby Pablo's face. It had the desired effect. Pablo was alive.

Pablo was baptised a Catholic at the Church of Santiago in Malaga, on the 10th of November in 1881. Though he later became a firm atheist, those close to him have claimed he had something of an obsession with faith, and his multiple superstitions attest to this. Later works, such as 1932's La Crucifixion, and in fact all his crucifixion paintings (and there are a few) also highlight his secret obsession with Christ and his demise. By the time he painted his famous crucifixion picture though, Picasso was in his fifties and in the midst of a most turbulent year. Some have said his crucifixion works were a kind of "remedy for artist's block", but Picasso was clearly fascinated with the whole idea of Christ sacrificing himself for man, just as the bull was viciously sacrificed during the bullfight. Indeed, sacrifice was important to Picasso; women were sacrificed at his alter in the name of art, and in a fashion Jose was to sacrifice his own artistic aspirations when he put all his faith into young Pablo.

The world now knows him as Pablo Picasso, but his birth name was actually Pablo Diego Jose Francisco de Paula Juan Nepomuceno Maria de los Remedios Cipriano de la Santisima Trinidad Ruiz y Picasso. Those numerous middle names derive from his late uncle, his grandfather, his father, his mother's father, his godfather, and his godmother. The latter, Maria, was breast feeding Pablo at the time, as

19

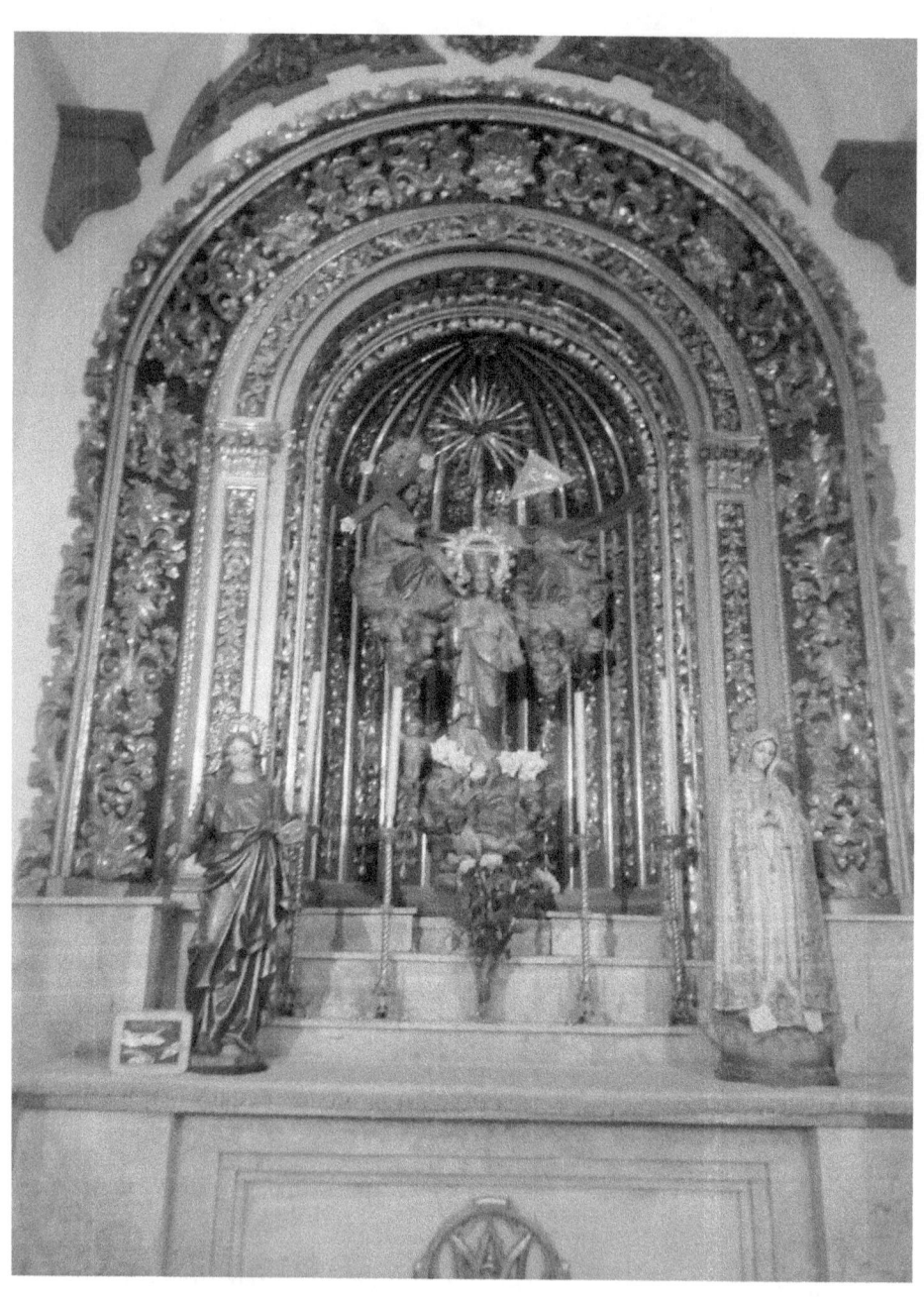

The Santiago Church, Malaga.

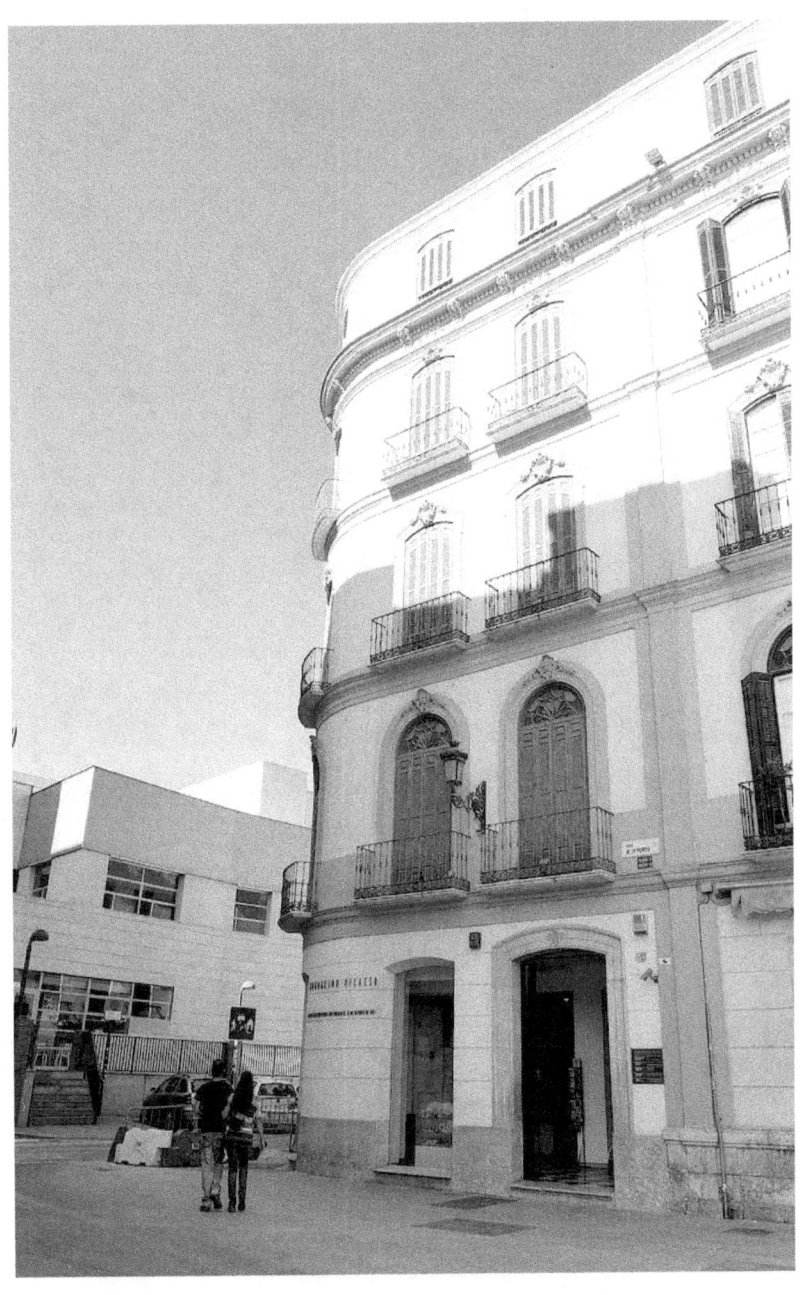

Picasso's birthplace, Malaga, Spain.

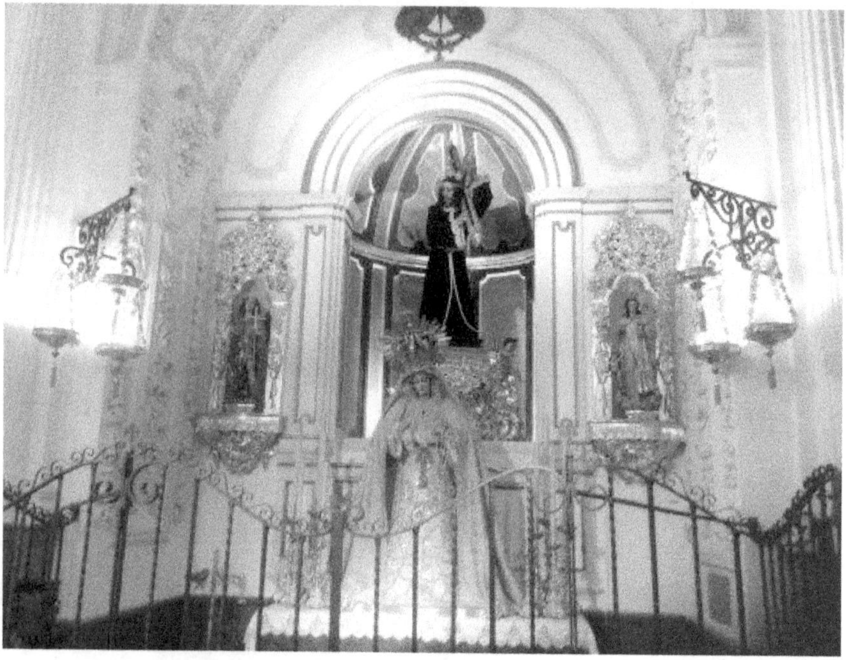

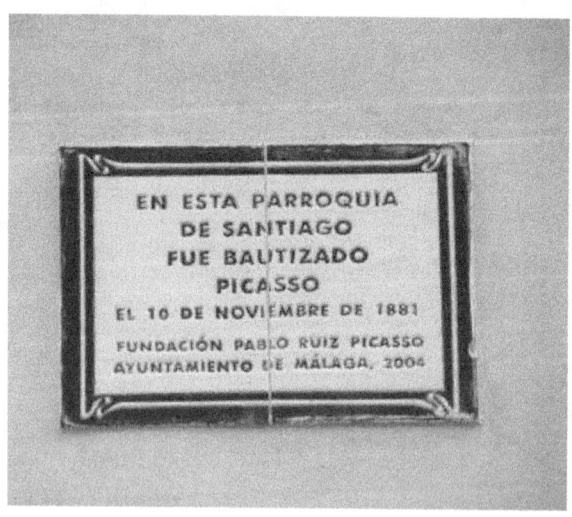

Above, the church in Malaga where Pablo Picasso was baptised.
Below, the plaque detailing his baptism.

EN ESTA PARROQUIA
DE SANTIAGO
FUE BAUTIZADO
PICASSO
EL 10 DE NOVIEMBRE DE 1881
FUNDACIÓN PABLO RUIZ PICASSO
AYUNTAMIENTO DE MÁLAGA, 2004

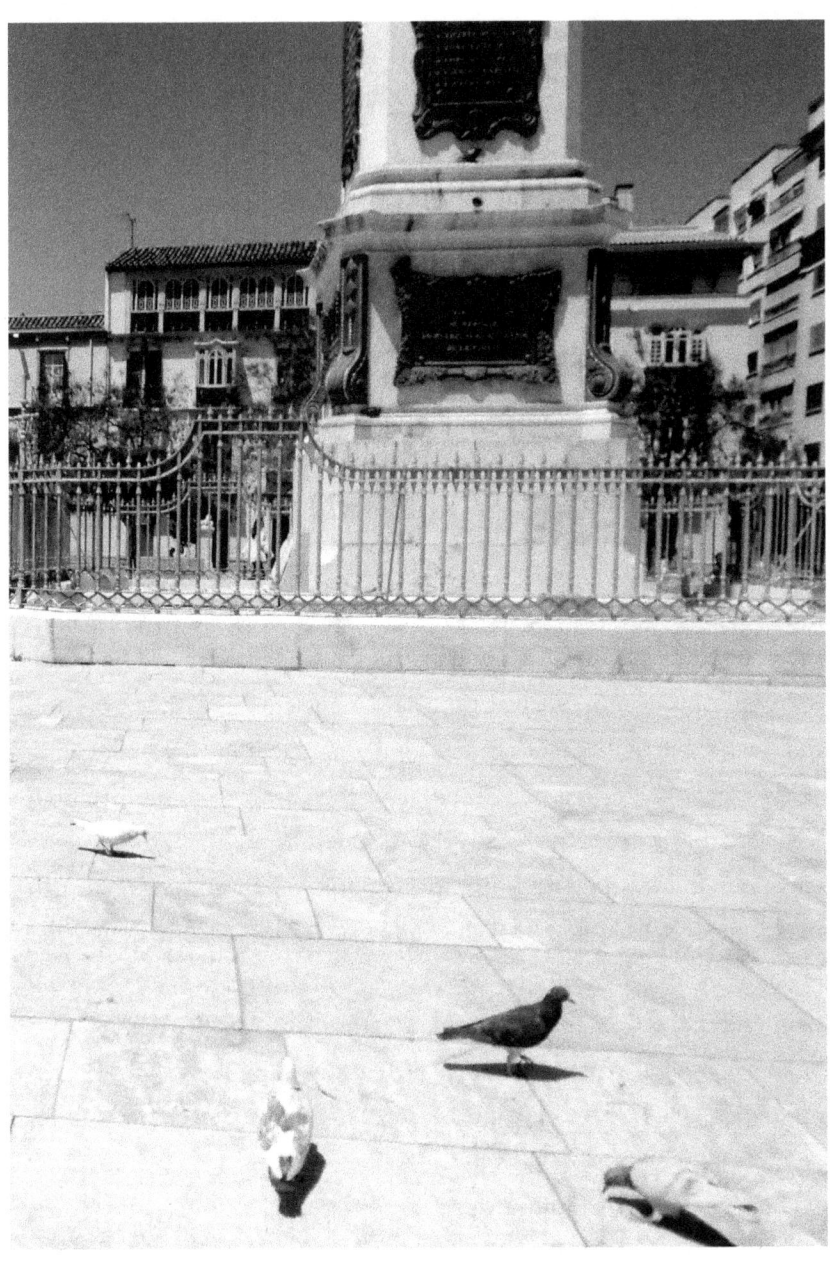

Pigeons near Picasso's birthplace. Photo taken by the author.

Pablo's mother had been left too exhausted by the traumatic birth to fulfil this role.

Pablo was named after his uncle, a well known doctor of theology who suddenly dropped dead three years before Picasso was born. The loss of Jose's brother was a serious issue in the family, especially for his two younger unmarried sisters who he supported financially. The death of the man was also symbolic; he was a God amongst them, and his connection to and avid interest in the Holy proved a comforting certainty in their lives. When he died, their whole world was rocked. One might say their belief in God himself might have been questioned, just as Pablo's would later be when a particularly traumatic event forced him to question what was really going on in the so called heavens above.

Usually, the life of a famous figure's parent is rather unimportant, uninteresting even. With Picasso it's the opposite; his father Jose, and to a lesser extent his mother, are vital characters in the artist's long story. Uncle Pablo had been a pillar of the community, and though Jose was no outcast, he was very different from the brother who encouraged and supported him. Jose adored painting and was much more introverted and reserved, known as the Englishman around Malaga for his pale skin and dark blond hair. But he was also a jovial man and a practical joker. There's a great story which concerns him buying an egg from a market seller, "eating" it raw and then producing a coin from his mouth, an act he repeated numerous times in a row, much to the delight of the trader.

Though well liked, and a keen socialiser to a degree, art was his passion. He would sit with other Malaga based artists in cafes, discussing the history of art. Yet he was at his happiest when at work

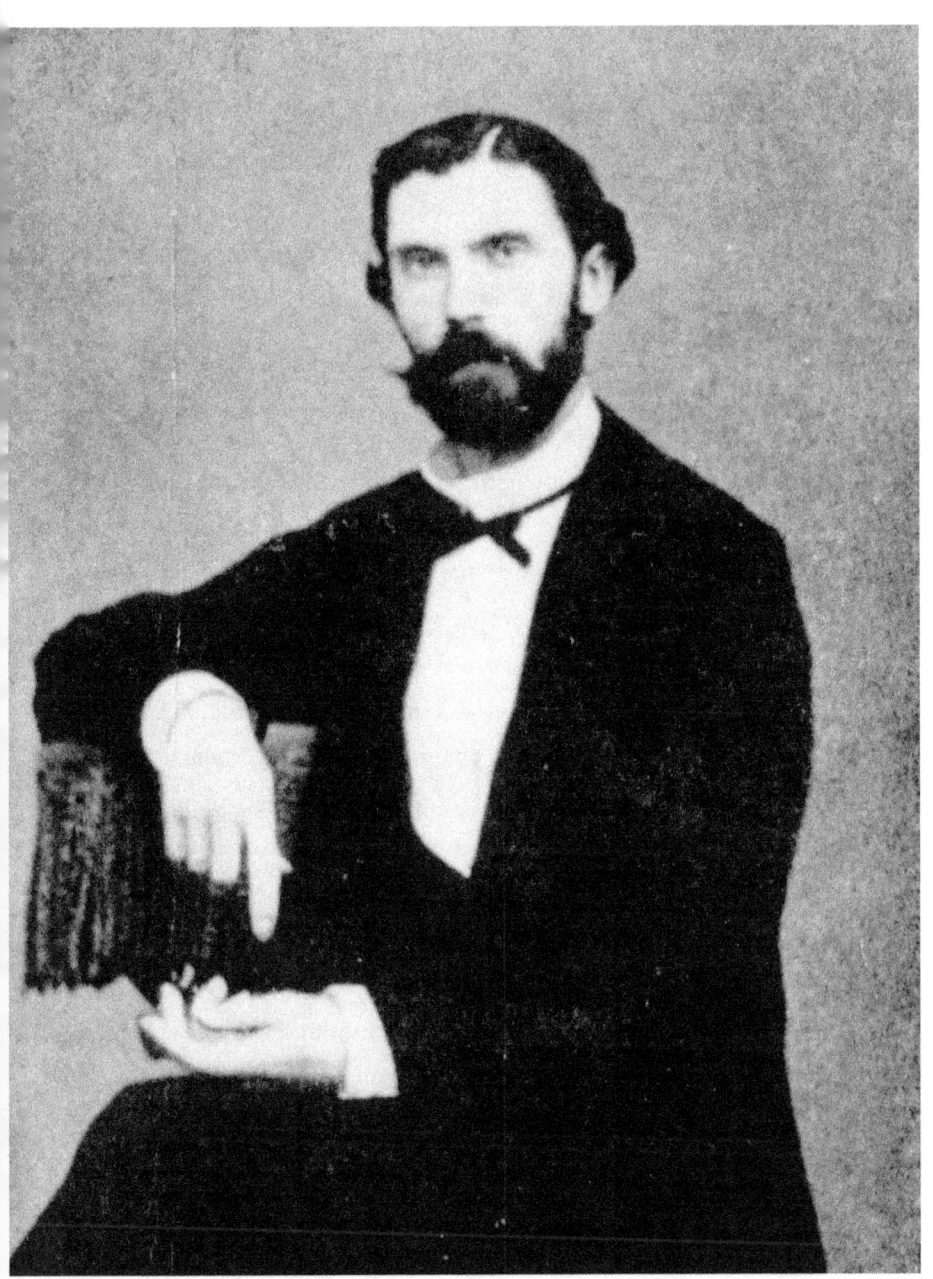

Picasso's father Jose, an artist and art teacher.

on his paintings. He taught art through the day, but it was when standing before a blank canvas, and seeing it fill with colour, that Jose came alive.

But with his heroic brother dead, Jose was left alone with his doubts; the doubts of his talent, his future, his destiny. Thankfully, Jose was not left out in the wilderness alone. He had met his future wife Maria, the woman who would bear him his children, young Pablo Picasso being the first to arrive. In name sake at least, Jose's brother lived on through his son, the little boy upon whom he had so much riding.

Jose and Maria had married in December of 1880, at the same church Pablo was baptised two years later. When he did arrive, Pablo lived a life surrounded by women, who pampered and fussed him like a young prince. His mother was always there by his side while Jose was at work, along with the female maid, while Pablo also regularly saw his grandmother and two aunts. As Malaga was in something of an economical drought, Jose wasn't just supporting his newborn son, but the women at home too. As well as teaching art, he had thankfully won the job of curator of the Malaga museum in 0, though this role was taken from him when they abruptly felt a curator was no longer needed. As teaching wasn't remarkably well paid, he made ends meet by selling his paintings, with the Malaga Town Hall famously buying one depicting his favourite animals, pigeons. Jose was the one with most of the pressure resting on him. To his relief, and after serious negotiations, he was reinstated as curator. As a bonus, he was also given space there to do his paintings, which came in handy seeing as there was such little space at home. To lighten his load further, the landlord at the Plaza de la Merced was lenient with the rent, and would often take Jose's paintings in place of cash if he was particularly hard up.

Maria was hopelessly proud of her son, calling him an angel and devil in beauty, insisting that passersby could not resist staring at him, this striking baby she held above all others. She instilled confidence in Picasso by praising him constantly as if he were some God sent gift, telling him: "If you are a soldier you will be a general, if you are a priest you will be a Pope." However much he adored it, he was not to be the sole subject of attention for much longer. When he was two, Pablo's sister Lola arrived. Shortly before her birth, Malaga had suffered a huge earthquake, and quite naturally Pablo connected these two traumatic events in his life. Forever, Lola was the bringer of this earth shattering natural disaster, destined to distract his mother who had been doting on him constantly since his birth. Still, as time went on, Pablo remained the family's bright light of hope.

When the news of the forthcoming earthquake was announced, the family left their cosy home for the safety of Antonio Degrain's house, an artist friend of Jose's who was away in Rome at the time, in order to avoid the full onslaught of its rampage. "My mother was wearing a kerchief on her head," Picasso recalled, "I had never seen her like that. My father grabbed his cape from the rack, threw it over himself, picked me up in his arms and wound me in its folds, leaving only my head exposed." In the midst of the upheaval Lola was born, and Pablo was no longer the baby. He had to share the spotlight, for now at least.

Another incident, or at least his perception of it, occurred around this time and had a huge impact on Picasso. Again, it was two separate happenings, coincidentally coinciding together, but in his wide eyed naivety Picasso saw them as one. As Antonio returned from Rome to the home Picasso and his family were occupying, King Alfonso XII visited Malaga. Picasso recalled the sight of Antonio appearing alongside the banners welcoming the arrival of the king, the carriages and smartly dressed men lining the streets. Naturally, Picasso thought they were celebrating his father's friend, the artist, completely unaware of the king's presence. To him then, at the tender age of two, an artist was someone to admire and worship, whose very being sent ordinary folk into rapture. It would prove to be a landmark association. Picasso himself would later court such hysteria when he visited a city or town, complete with his entourage,

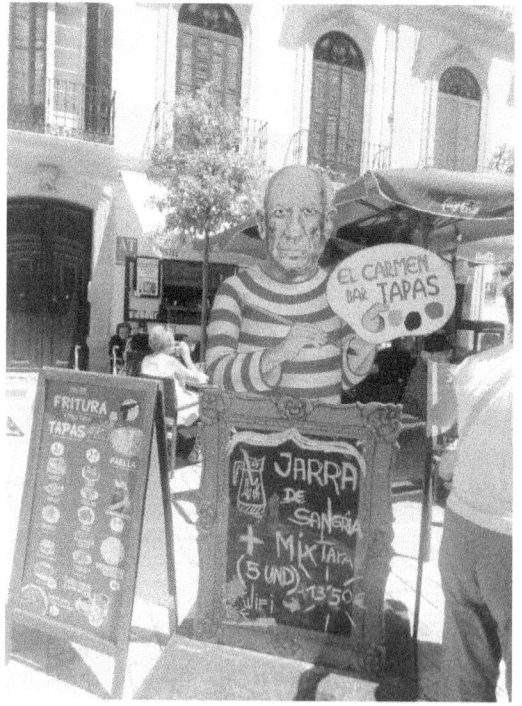

Picasso's legend looms large in Malaga today. Photos by the author, 2017.

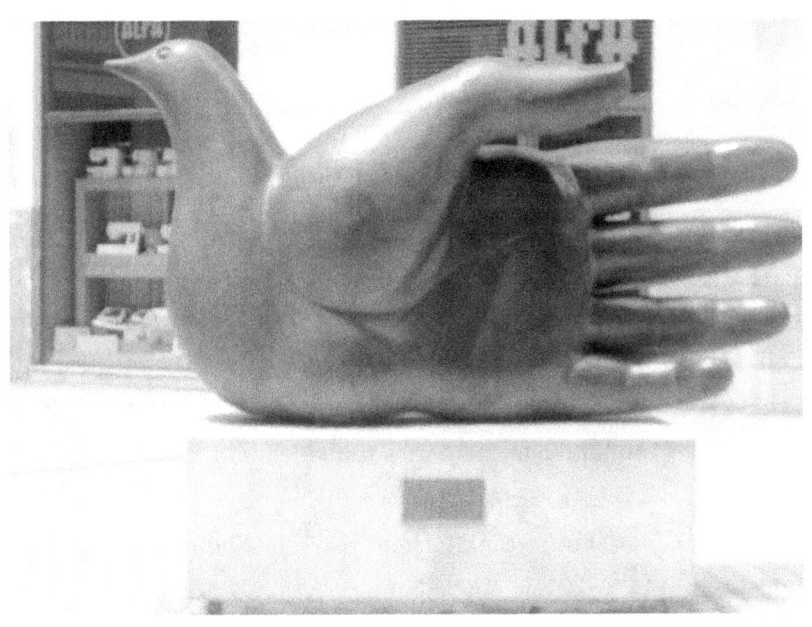

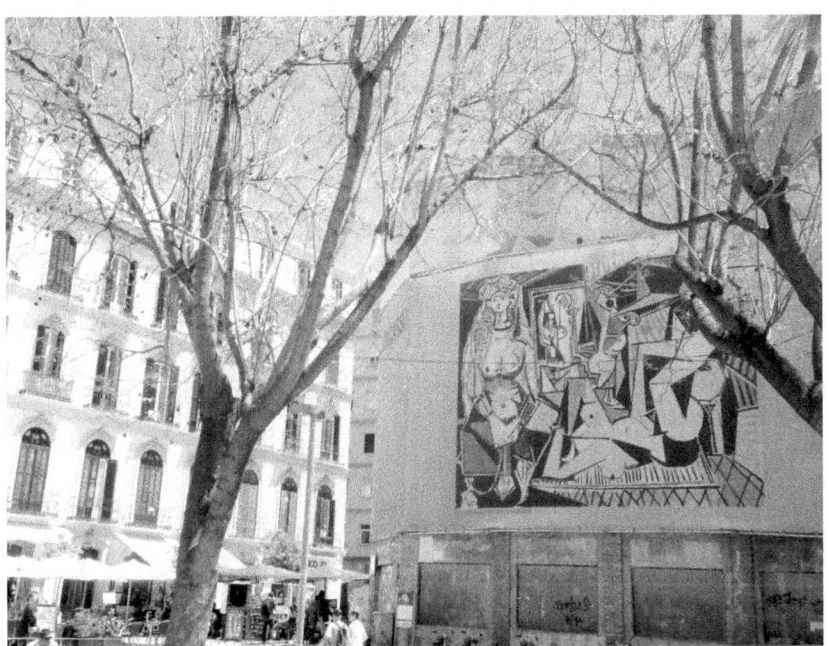

Malaga scenes, including a bird of peace. Photos by the author.

and his appearance was treated like that of a king, a figure to honour and bow before. Malaga's favourite son was already having big ideas when he saw the mass applause and the hero's welcome.

His first word was piz (short in Spanish for lapiz, i.e. pencil) and it's been said he could draw before he could walk. "Piz" he would demand, and within seconds his fussing mother would hand him his instrument of choice. As was clear from later recollections, these early Malagan childhood memories remained with him forever. His love of the spirally caracola buns became a minor part of his myth, the treats served hot in the Malagan market. When Pablo wanted a bun he simply drew one, and his mother immediately followed his order. Art then, always got him what he wanted. Pablo also recalled the walks on the beach with his father, collecting and saving shells, fascinated by their varying shapes. Even at such a young age, he was transfixed by form. Only later would he learn to redefine our concept of physicality.

With pencil in hand, Picasso first drew shapes, but by the age of four he was sketching animals, creatures which seemed to come from nowhere, and more traditionally, flowers, again being struck by their varied forms. He would complete art works to order, and his mother often suggested donkeys. "Now what?" he would ask, ready and willing to conjure up more magic from thin air. It seems he was born with that magic gift. In later footage of Picasso, particularly in the startling 1950 film Mystery of Picasso, you can see the assured confidence in his line, his effortless ease with the pencil, creating his simplistic winding roads of creativity with pure control, meeting them up to form life forms and figures, bulls and beauties.

Pablo hated school. Being so creative and free at home, and enjoying life at his own pace, rather predictably he found educational structure boring and constricting. An anti authoritarian, he would shun the teachers and go to the window, hand signalling to his aunt's husband, Antonio, to come and collect him. "One," he would mime, meaning one hour, the least amount of time to wait. He would arrive, right on cue, after an hour, and take young Pablo for a walk. The only subject he was interested in learning about was art, and even then it was to his own guidelines only.

Thankfully, Jose was OK with that. Art was what it was all about after all. For hours Pablo would watch his father paint, enraptured by his technique and the wizardry appearing on the canvases. He viewed his depiction of pigeons as something magical, as if the bird, considered a pest everywhere else in the world, were a God among the other animals. Even in later years when the world thought he was drawing doves, it was really pigeons. Of course, his attachment to pigeons came from the worship of his father. Again, he associated these two things as one. When he later spoke in wonderment of a particular picture his father did of a group of pigeons, found in the museum of Malaga years later, it was anything but the "enormous" masterpiece Picasso had hailed it. Like all children, he tended to aggrandise memories into something much more monumental. But he adored his father, of that there is no doubt. When Jose walked him to school, Picasso insisted on taking the stuffed pigeon with him which his dad used for his paintings. Picasso would plonk it on his desk and draw it all day, ignore whatever the teacher was going on about and wait for his father's appearance at the door. As his father needed the pigeon for his work, he was certain he'd return. Manipulation became another key factor in his daily life.

In the end however, when Picasso began to throw tantrums and refuse to go inside, he was transferred to a private school, where they were more sensitive to his needs, his refusal to absorb any education unless it was to do with art. At the Colegio de San Rafael, he followed the headmaster's wife around "like a puppy". Already, he had an insatiable interest in the fairer sex. He was occasionally tutored at home, if the money permitted, and on schooling days was allowed to take the maid into class with him, where she'd hold the pigeon for him to draw. Clearly, Picasso the prince knew how to bend things to his advantage.

Yet he was a poor student, unable to grasp the simplest tasks, such as reading or even the flow of numbers. His blamed his inability to count on the fact that "one" was essentially the time his father would come and pick him up and take him home. "It didn't sink in," he recalled, "don't think I didn't try." He would attempt to count, but always come back to one o'clock. His mind was on the clock, as were his eyes, and he watched it obsessively; "like an idiot" he claimed, waiting for home-time to arrive. Whether Picasso's inability to absorb even the most basic of education was down to a genuine learning difficulty or his obsessive desire to draw is a question for the ages, but as far as it seems to me, it was probably the latter. Art was so important to him that everything else, save women, paled in comparison, especially school.

Outside his unsatisfying life in the class room, a second sister came along in October 1887, Concepcion, with Uncle Salvador, the good omen who had revived Pablo with the cigar smoke, as her godfather.

It's hard to say what Picasso's earliest art was like, but judging by the reactions of family members it must have been exceptional for a young boy. However, his earliest works, at least the ones that have survived, do not display a particularly unique talent, at least not the very early material. Pablo once said "I never drew like a child, I drew like Raphael." But that was far from the truth. One of his earliest surviving artworks, Hercules with his Club, drawn in 1890 at the age of 9, is anything but like the work of Raphael. To his credit, he was not even ten years old yet, but the proportions of the picture are wrong and there is nothing exceptional about the whole thing. Pablo though, typically, remembered it as something much grander.

"I still remember one of my first drawings," he said, "In the passage at home, there was a picture of Hercules with his club. One day I sat down in the passage and drew this Hercules. But it was not a child's drawing. It was a true drawing and a real representation of that Hercules, club and all." John Richardson, Picasso's legendary biographer, later called it "rather inept."

Hercules with the Club is not the first major example of Picasso's talent. Earlier pictures include the Port of Malaga which he painted in around 1888, and the most important from the early years, the charming one of the bullring he did with oil in 1889. It was a picture he kept in his personal collection all his life. The sentimentality he felt for it, and the unbreakable attachment, was not just related to the fact it was an early painting, but because Pablo adored bullfighters as a boy, and he had treasured memories at the Malaga bullring. His father was friends with a famous bullfighter called Carancha, and he would often visit the family's house. Pablo would sit on his knee and idolise the man. Picasso also recalled that he was once so desperate to touch a bullfighter's "suit of lights" that he cried until he was allowed to do so. He was utterly transfixed.

To encourage practise, Picasso's father gave him sketchbooks, inside which he honed his craft and doodled for hours. In one of these is a vital sheet; at the top of the page, there are five pigeons, wonderfully captured (Jose must have been very pleased), and if you turn the page round, the other end reveals a romantically presented bullfight scene, with three matadors, a raging bull and crowd of spectators. If one piece of paper could sum up Picasso's childhood then it is this. It has to be said also that they are two of the things which remained endlessly fascinating to Picasso throughout his whole life. Indeed, the bullfight and its bloodthirsty ritual is present in some form or another in many of his key paintings. Guernica may be depicting the horrendous massacre of the small Spanish town, bombed to dust and debris in 1937, but in the midst of the horror scene Picasso has included a bull and a sacrificed horse. To him, the bullfight was everything, and it could represent life itself, a bloody battle of which there is no escape, where one has to face ones' fears. And the birds remained vital to him, whether in the mouth of a feral cat, or representative of freedom in the dove of peace.

At this age Pablo was showing future signs of greatness and Jose was ecstatic and hopeful about his future. Claude Picasso, Pablo's son to Francoise Gilot, once said, "He (Pablo) was the best student his father ever had." Bernard Ruiz Picasso, Picasso's grandson, later added that Jose was "not only astonished but petrified by the talent of his son." There is truth in both statements.

There was no oedipal complexity when it came to Pablo and Jose. Jose worshipped him and he worshipped him back. Subconsciously, as Freud might have later argued, there may have been some strange emotions beneath the surface - a little jealousy from Jose perhaps, but so crushed down it was impossible to truly feel - but it seems to have been a healthy relationship; until Pablo wished to defy his father's obsessions with academic painting. And Pablo's relationship with his stocky, sturdy mother seems to have had no dark qualities either; she doted on him and he in turn enjoyed it.

Life in Malaga was perfect, but all good things come to an end. It was at the end of 1890 that the family had to leave Malaga. The decision was not made lightly, but out of sheer necessity. The museum was about to close down, meaning José would be out of work. Pablo was devastated, but José had to go where the money was. He saw a post for a drawing teacher at the Da Guarda Institute in the Spanish port city of A Coruna and immediately applied for it. Though they would be leaving, Malaga, the place he was born and spent his first nine years, would never leave his heart.

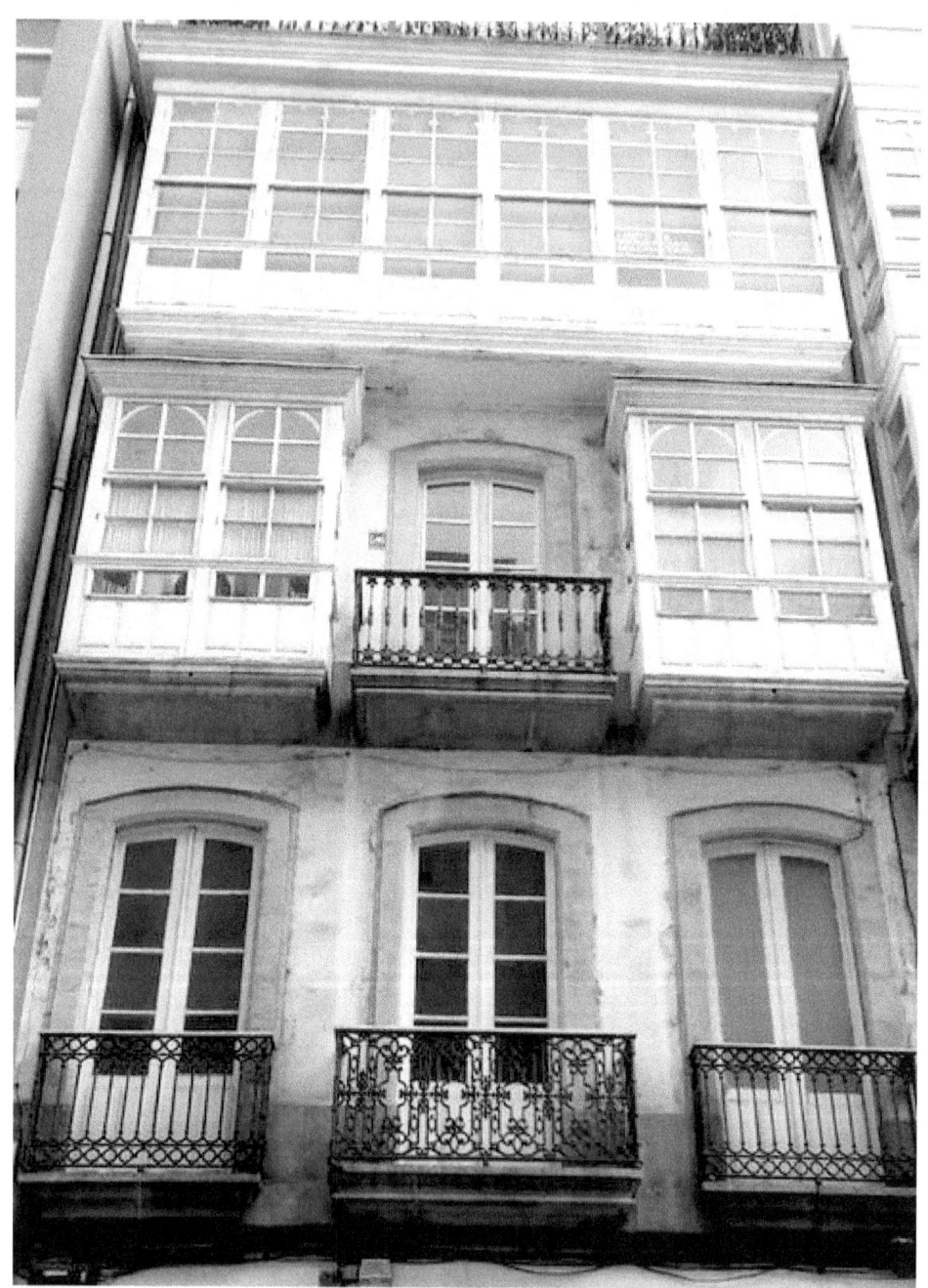

Picasso's childhood home in A Coruna.

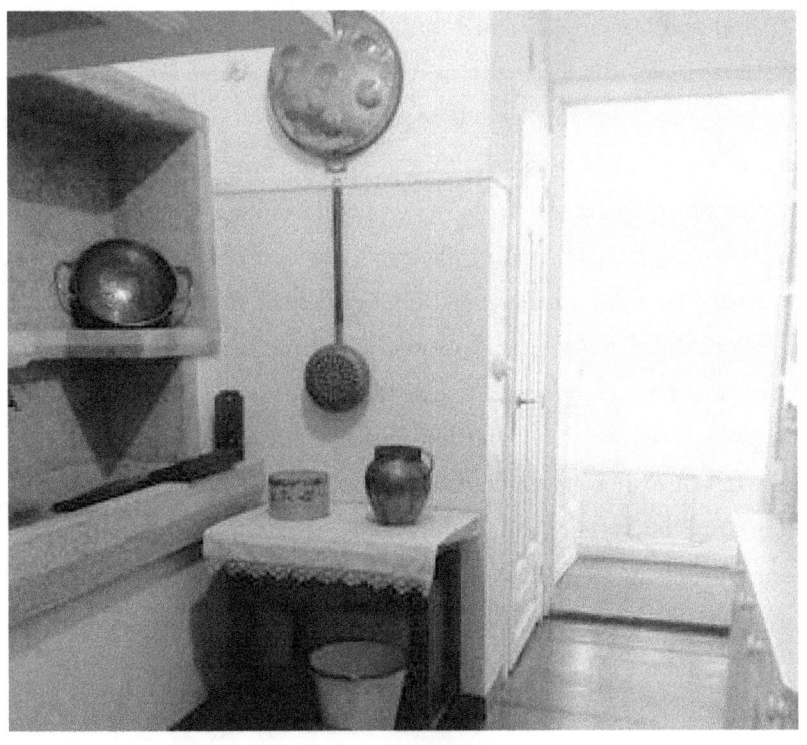

"I'LL SHOW THEM WHAT I CAN DO!"

Life in A Coruna: 1891 - 1895

The second chapter of Picasso's life takes us to A Coruna, a coastal city at the very North of Spain, as far away from the Southern comforts of Malaga as it's possible to get within the country. Picasso was saddened to say goodbye to his birth home and all the locations and sights that were a part of his daily childhood life. But Jose could not be picky, and when his application was accepted in A Coruna, the family had no choice but to relocate.

Pablo and his family stayed in A Coruna for four years, from 1891 to 1895. In all the Picasso eras, this is the one that seems the least explored, yet in many ways it is as important as his days in Malaga and other eras to follow. His time there saw him from the age of 10 to almost 14, essentially from being a child to a teenager. It is easy to fall into the trap of dividing Picasso's life into chapters, segments if you will, because it tidies up the biographical time line of his long journey. Such over simplification can usually mean whole time frames are hopped over because they seem less relevant, but in Picasso's case, every era and location is as important as the next or last. In A Coruna, he made particular advancements as an artist. He didn't find his style or indeed himself (that would happen in 1901, as many people agree), but he did make some leaps. Perhaps this should be named the "A Coruna Period"...

The problem with his time in A Coruna is that it is not particularly characteristic. Picasso folk lore has allowed us to colour in each era with a simplistic phrase that doesn't cover the whole time frame but at least summarises the strongest elements from it; Malaga is the true childhood place; Paris at the turn of the new century is where he discovers life itself; 1901 to 1906 are commonly referred to as the Blue and Rose periods, even though many other moods and colours do sneak into his oeuvre in the work; 1907 to the teens are his Cubist period, in which he explored this new radical art form with Georges Braque; the twenties are his classicalist, society years with Olga Khokhlova... and so on. Yet A Coruna is sidelined. Maybe it's because it's a plain (yet no less beautiful and vibrantly busy) port town way up north, that it doesn't have the glamour of other Picasso related destinations, like the earthy machismo of Malaga or the art hub heaven that is Paris.

Before the family arrived in A Coruna, Jose put Pablo forward for his test to see him into secondary school. Knowing full well that Pablo would not be able to pass it alone, and given his vital connections in Malaga, Jose knew that now was the time to pull the necessary strings to get his son through, something he would not be able to do as an unknown in A Coruna. The examiner asked Jose, "What does he know?" Jose looked to his son and bluntly replied, "Nothing." It was harsh but true.

When the test began, Picasso was unable to focus on the simplistic tasks at hand. "You can't imagine what I suffered trying to pay attention," he recalled years later, "I'd be distracted by the thought that it was necessary to pay attention and this would confuse me." Still unable to pass the most basic of tests, the examiner kindly simplified it further, as a favour to Jose, in order for Picasso to grasp what was asked of him. Jose had promised Picasso that if he passed he would be allowed to do an oil painting. In the end, the examiner let Pablo look at the answers and copy them. He left with a diploma which would allow him access to the secondary school in A Coruna. "I'll show them what I can do," he insisted on his journey home.

As he turned ten (or was about to, depending on sources) the family finally took the ship to A Coruna; Pablo, Lola, Concepcion, Jose and Maria, away from the guiding lights and figures of great comfort who had made life easier and supported them in various ways.

As it turns out, A Coruna was no match for Malaga; hot, familiar, warm in tone, compared to A Coruna's poor weather, fog and depressing air. They were strangers in a strange land, and Jose was desperately unhappy there.

"In Coruna," Picasso said, "my father did not leave the house except to go to the School of Arts and Crafts (to teach). He returned home and amused himself painting, but not so much anymore. The rest of the time he spent watching the rain through the windowpanes. No Malaga, no friends, no bulls, nothing."

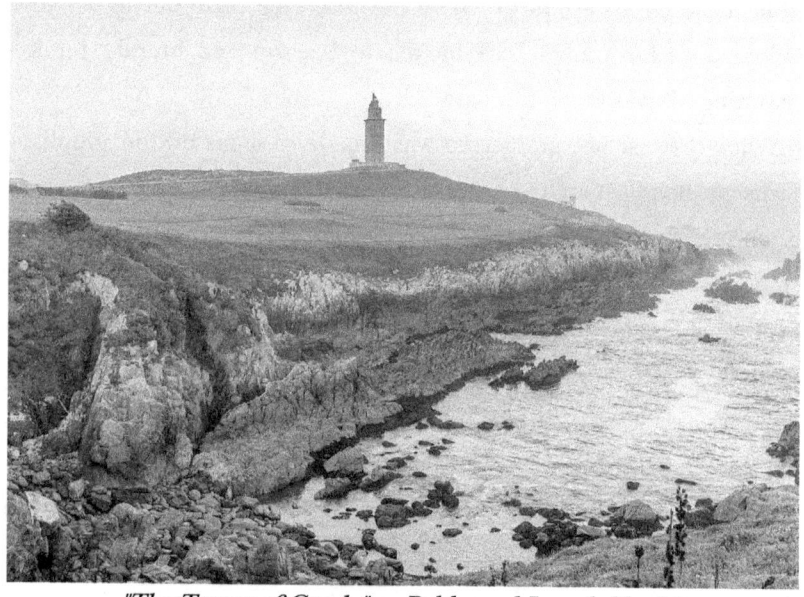

"The Tower of Candy" as Pablo and Jose dubbed it,
on the coast of A Coruna.

Picasso may have been romanticising Jose's dark feelings at the time, but it's highly likely he was feeling so blue. After all, his whole livelihood, security and reputation had been robbed of him. No longer was he able to sit with his friends discussing art in the cafes, go to the brothel or enjoy the passionate bull fights at the Malaga bull ring. A Corruna held nothing for him, except a job.

Pablo himself though seems to have had a good time in A Coruna, bonding with class mates and staging mock bull fights where one of them would act as the horned creature. Pablo's mother tried to keep a close eye on her son while he was playing with his gang, having pretend shoot outs with toy guns, but she could not see the furthest reaches of the street; for that, Picasso remembered "she had to stand on her tiptoe on the toilet seat to watch me play through the tiny bathroom window." Ever the myth maker, Picasso made the everyday activity of playing with friends sound like some blissfully painted scenario.

At school he drew constantly, just as distracted in class as he had been in Malaga. At one point he even wrote a raunchy poem in the margin of his school book, which concerned a female donkey lifting her tail and the male brute driving in his nail. Punishment at school was being sent to a white cell with nothing but a bench. Naturally, Pablo loved it there, especially if he could take a pad and pencil with him. He'd spend his confinement time practising his craft. "I could be isolated there with no one bothering me, drawing, drawing, drawing," he remembered.

In September of 1892, almost a year into their time in A Coruna, Jose enrolled Pablo at the School of Fine Arts to begin his formal training. He was only ten, but Jose knew it was vital for him to go to classes if he were to become the great academic painter he wished him to be. Lo and behold, Pablo was accepted, and ended up in his own father's class. Works do survive from this era, where Picasso was drawing bust figures and learning about the structure of the human body. Pablo was a good student there, faithfully following the rules for once, and enjoying himself no end. He received good grades and his drawings showed signs of special talent. For the first time perhaps, Jose was not worried about his son's future. He was always proud, but as a man full of doubt, he perhaps secretly feared what would become of him. Now he was not so concerned.

One early story in A Coruna, which many deny is true, involves Jose giving Picasso a brush, some paints and a blank canvas, and leaving two severed pigeon feet on the side for him to copy. He left him to it and went out. Upon his return, Jose was so struck by the authentic quality of his son's work that Jose handed him his paints, said he didn't need them himself anymore, and vowed never to paint again. In reality of course Jose *did* paint again. After all, he was a firm and disciplined artist, and this was not enough to put an end to his passion. (That would come later.)

As his father and teacher, Jose saw much promise in young Pablo, and through him, his sharp eyed boy, he could live out his own unachieved goals. As mentioned, Jose wanted Picasso to become a well known academic painter, and he held this view all the way to Pablo's adulthood. To him, this was the ultimate position in art, a well paid job within the establishment. Of course, Pablo *would* become an artist, but he would do it his way, completely defying Jose's rules of tradition.

In his A Coruna based sketchbooks, Picasso drew Hercules once again, and now he had a firmer grasp on the human structure, the work was more assured and accomplished. 1892 also has Picasso returning again and again to the bullfight. Some of his surviving sketches of the battles are extraordinarily good for a ten year old and they evoke a sense of awe, both for the blood sport and Picasso's abilities. His birds are equally good, as is one particularly strong sketch of a bearded man in profile dating from 1892 or possibly 93. Still, either way, the oldest he could have been when doing these works was eleven. Study For A Torso also shows how he could bring an ordinary drawing subject to life, enhancing the straight forward figure and bringing it off the page.

His bullfight sketches, though not radically different in presentation from his earlier depictions, are much more accomplished in their details and perspective. These early books are a gift to the Picasso student, for in many ways studies, outlines and rough sketches show the development of an artist more thoroughly than finished paintings often do. In Picasso's case, they show his obsession with art and how at this point his fascination remained in the bull ring. Indeed, there are no females yet, it's important to note.

In 1893 he finished Farmhouse, an oil on canvas piece which betrayed his youth and appeared as a very accomplished work in its own right. Clearly, the lessons were paying off, as was the dedicated practise. He also made his own newspaper complete with illustrations and caricatures, did plaster copies of ancient sculptures and began working on more serious pieces which showed a proper development of his skills. House in the Countryside, done in 1893, also shows his style was still more concerned with realism, and his work resembles a later hero of his, Vincent Van Gogh. Eerily it seems that the still obscure ghost of Vincent was hovering over Pablo, and his own style (or styles) had not yet come to the fore.

At the end of 1894 he painted a fabulous portrait of his sister Lola, a work which considering he was just entering his teens should have convinced those around him he had a serious future and was perhaps a prodigious genius. His first masterpiece, though some might not claim it to be one, is the Barefoot Girl, painted in A Coruna in 1895. The sad face of the little girl is what strikes us the most, those empty, large, black eyes. Even though the picture has some fine details in it - the cloth draped over her shoulder, the crossed hands, the red dress, the bare feet of course - it's the mournful eyes which penetrate the observer, making one feel almost guilty for merely gazing at her. Just like some of his later landmark works, it's when the subject stares back at us that we feel an immediate sense of attachment to the work, both aesthetic and emotional. It isn't always a nice feeling (he could leave that to the more commercial Impressionists), but it's an involving one, which is very important. The fact he did the Barefoot Girl painting at the mere age of 13 is astounding. Clearly, A Coruna was more a vital place in his development than many Picasso historians let on.

The year 1895 is Picasso's strongest up to that date. His academic studies of the body are advancing fast, while his landscapes are breathtakingly accomplished. He was still rooted firmly in realism, but he was giving the subjects an extra dimension, a soul almost. His mournful portrait of his mother is exceptional, capturing her in a pensive mood, while his painting of Clipper the dog is beautiful, though one would never guess it was a Picasso work at all.

Picasso may have literally been born in Malaga, as a human being coming into the physical world, but his artistic awakening and rebirth if you like definitely occurred in A Coruna. It was here he learned at least some discipline and began to grasp the human form, understood the tools he had for executing his vision and how art could be the finest form of expression.

In other areas outside art Picasso was growing up fast. He had his first love in A Coruna, Angeles Mendez Gill, a girl in his class who he became besotted with. He doodled romanticised in his sketchbooks, using his and her initials in blissful drawings, as children often do when in love, entwining their names as one. Unfortunately, the girl's family did not approve of Pablo's interest in their daughter. They were from very different classes to start with; Gill's family were almost upper class, while Pablo's were lower middle class, coming from the south of Spain of all places. The Northern Spaniards looked down on the Andalusians (consider Dali and Bunuel's landmark surreal movie, An Andalusian Dog, for example), especially if they were from a "lower" social standing to them.

Despite the barriers, Pablo and Angeles began sending each other innocent love letters, but her parents were so keen to fight off Pablo's advances that they sent her away to Pamplona. He was heartbroken by the loss and also deeply offended that he was deemed unfit for being too poor, "beneath" Angeles' family for social reasons alone. It might easily be hopped over in his time line, but Angeles may be the first Picasso muse (she appears in sketchbooks, but not any paintings), and his inability to "have" her may have led to some of his future views towards women and love; his possessiveness, his jealousy, his need to own and then discard the woman.

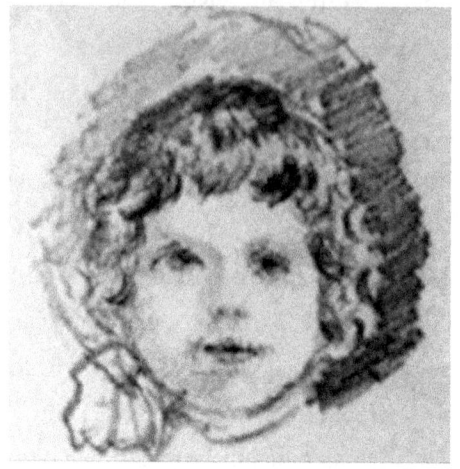

Picasso's sketch of his beloved sister Conchita, who died at the mere age of 9.

If Pablo thought the recent lost love had shaken his world, he did not anticipate the next earth shattering occurrence which came from nowhere and threatened the stability of his whole family. His sister Conchita, of whom he was particularly fond, suddenly fell ill with diphtheria. Young Pablo watched with helplessness as his little sister went gradually down hill, and the worry on the faces of his parents and Dr Costales troubled him. Jose and Maria tried to carry on as if nothing was wrong; Christmas went on as usual and Conchita had no idea she was about to die. Picasso was desperate for the Lord to save her, and so he made a bargain with the big man upstairs. If God were to spare her life, then Pablo would give up his beloved painting. Pablo was torn between the loyalty to his sister and the dedication to his art. He loved the latter, of that there is no doubt, but it's a testament to his adoration for Conchita that he would even think of giving up his calling. Unfortunately, he need not have worried about the loss of his art. Sadly, despite his pleas, God showed no mercy. Poor Conchita died at the age of 8 in 1895.

This is undoubtedly the incident which convinced Picasso that being an atheist was the only realistic way forward. Yes, some have claimed he still had faith and feared the wrath of God, but his respect for the Lord was no doubt damaged if not killed the day Conchita was taken to the skies. The death affected the whole family badly. It's been reported that José really did give up painting as a passionate hobby, and handed his supplies to Picasso. A piece of him had died when Conchita was cruelly snatched away from him, and from here on Jose seems to have gone down hill. By the time Picasso painted him in 1895, the year Conchita died, he appears sunken, gaunt and hopelessly sad, frail and sullen. In fact he resembles a Van Gogh self portrait, but the anguish in his eyes is certainly not contrived. This is a broken man. Picasso may not have been aware of the recently deceased artist's work, but it bares an uncanny resemblance. Still, it appears to be a coincidence and an accurate depiction of Jose at the time. (Picasso was definitely a fan of Van Gogh later on though, being directly influenced by him and others in his early Parisian days, and even carrying a newspaper cutting referencing Van Gogh's death.)

Perhaps seeing A Coruna as some cursed bad omen, and wanting a fresh start after this horrific incident, Jose requested another work transfer, this time to somewhere much more exciting and enticing to the young Pablo. In March, he exchanged jobs with a Barcelona based art teacher who wished to head home to A Coruna. But before they departed forever, Jose held a small exhibition in the back of a shop for young Pablo. For the first time, his works were shown to the public, and he was not yet even fourteen. He even sold a few works, much to his delight, as the patrons came and went in the umbrella shop out front.

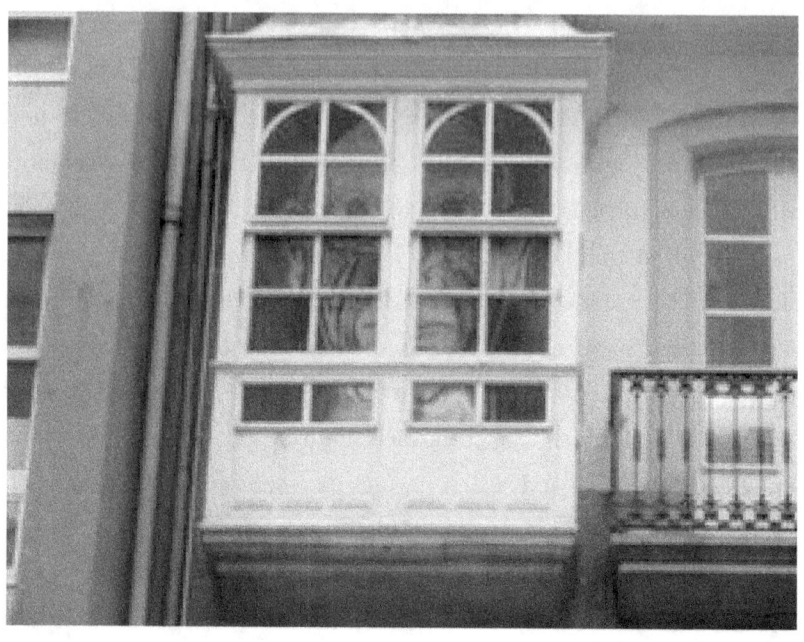

The window of the A Coruna apartment, now baring the face of Picasso himself, staring out at the world.

After the small exhibition, they headed back to Malaga by train, where they stayed at Uncle Salvador's house. In his four years absence, Picasso had improved as an artist no end and the Malagan relatives were more than a little impressed by his progress. At this stage, Picasso's work captured figures beautifully but somehow managed to bring forth their hidden emotions, their complexities, their problems. Yet he was still so young, barely in control of understanding his own emotions, never mind those of the needy, poor and downtrodden.

In this little time frame, Uncle Salvador seems to have come forward as an additional role model for Pablo. Yes, his father remained his hero, and Jose doted on Pablo's talents enthusiastically, but Salvador too, the very man who had revived him all those years earlier with the cigar smoke, was an enthusiastic patron and supporter. In that beautiful Malaga summer he even paid him to keep painting (the ultimate encouragement, and this from a man he respected enormously), hired him a live model and set him up in a little studio. Salvador also took him to bullfights, as long as he agreed to go to communion. "I would have gone to communion twenty times for a chance of going to the bullfight," he later exclaimed.

When the golden summer ended, Picasso and the family moved on to Barcelona, where they would enter yet another phase of their life. A Coruna may not have given them much positivity (in fact it had given them true horror), but for Picasso the artist it had been a learning curve. He had also learned first hand about love and true loss, the latter something the artist perversely gains from in his work. As important as A Coruna was, the following destination would be the place where it all truly kick-started into gear.

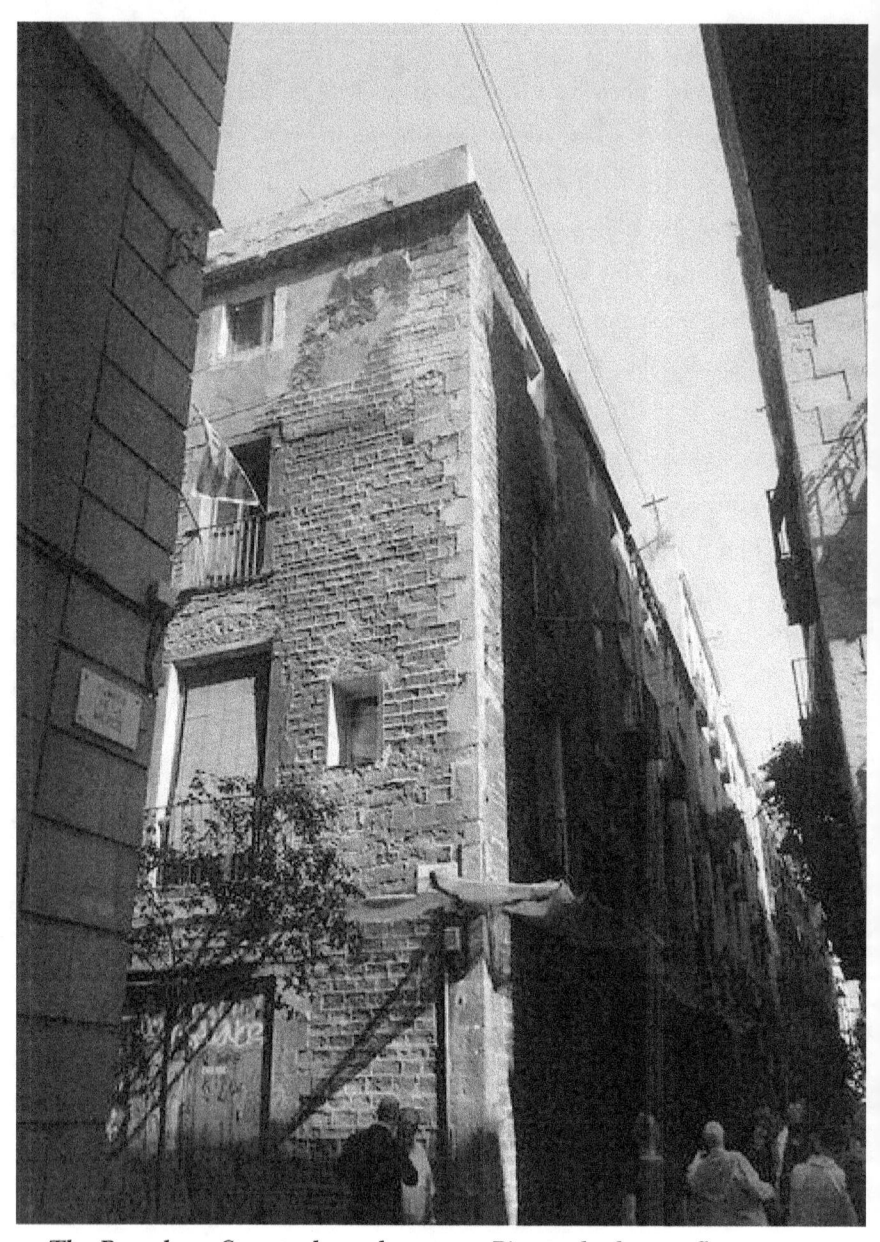

The Barcelona Street where the young Picasso had a top floor art studio, paid for by his father.

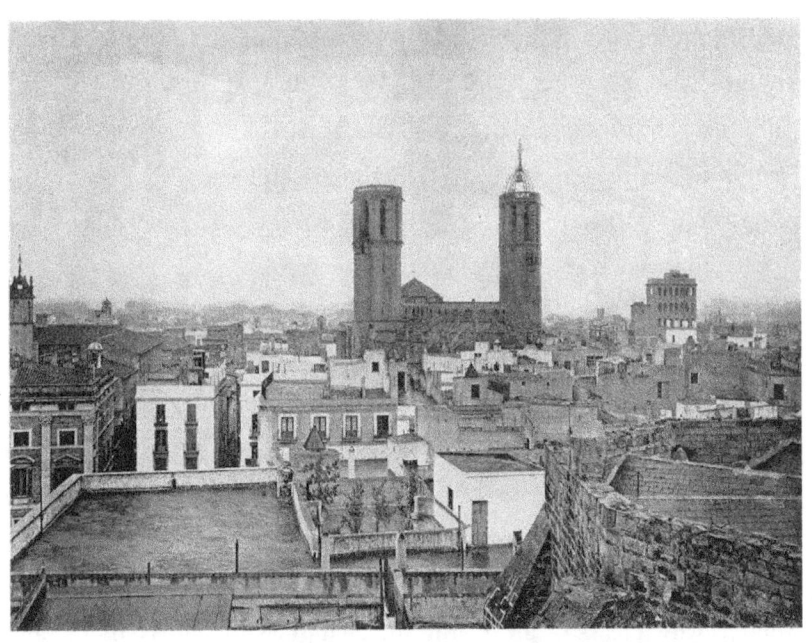

"HERE IS WHERE IT ALL BEGAN..."

Barcelona and Madrid

Seeing as the time spent in A Coruna is so often glossed over (especially in Picasso documentaries where it barely gets a mention), Barcelona is often considered to be the true birthplace of Picasso; not Pablo the young man, but Pablo Picasso the Great Artist. Barcelona's case for the destination where Picasso became Picasso is aided by the fact the man himself often spoke of the city as a hugely important place where he discovered his abilities. "Here is where it all began," he famously said. "This is where I realised where I could get to."

Jose was now teaching at the Llotja School of Fine Arts, and Pablo was a pupil there. It was a bit of a comedown for Picasso himself. In

Malaga during the summer he'd been something of a wunderkind, a prodigy lauded by his family who were dazzled and impressed by Pablo's capabilities and quick progress. In Barcelona however, with no friends to begin with, he was just another pupil, another face in the mass of crowds. But the Catalan city was a hugely exciting place to be, and Pablo loved every minute of his time there.

For one, the architecture must have pleased him, especially the work of modernist architect and designer Antoni Gaudi, who was at that time in the early stages of overseeing the construction of his astonishing Sagrada Familia cathedral, the towering monument to modern faith which is still seeing refurbishment to this day. It was in Barcelona that he first saw art outside the classicist rule book and came across alternative literature, politics and ideas. One may wonder why Picasso's art begins to change while he is living and studying in Barcelona, but it's actually quite simple. For the first time he was experiencing life and art which was outside his father's constricting influence.

Again, he did not enjoy being a student. During one exam, he decided to do it his way, regardless of what the feedback may be, in a bid to say "take me or leave me." In his eyes, the school needed him more than he needed the school. He was given a month to finish the drawings which they would be examining, but Picasso later claimed he did them all in one day. Picasso the anti authoritarian was at his most arrogant in Barcelona, but in his defence it was not a reluctance to follow orders, but a total and utter inability to do so. His mind worked in a way that meant if he didn't want to do something, he wouldn't do it. This extraordinary self belief led him to great things in the future, but as a teenaged art student it merely made enemies of his so called superiors.

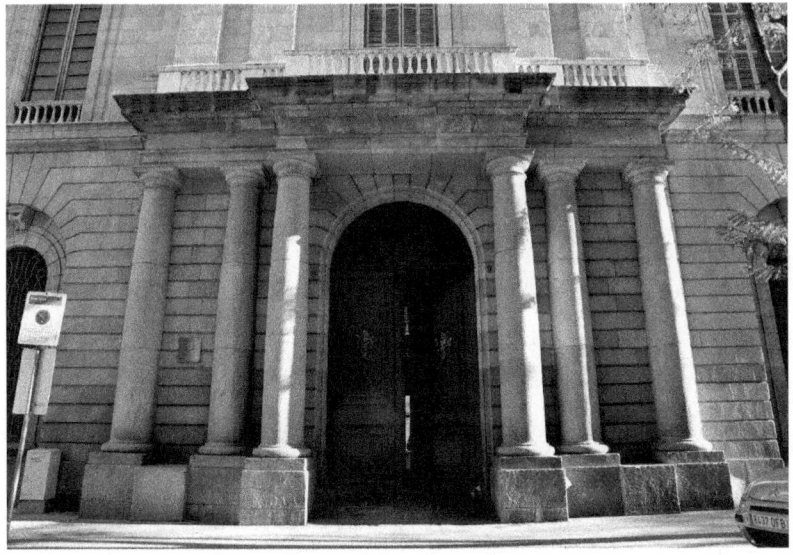

The Llotja School of Fine Arts, which young Picasso attended while living in Barcelona.

Barcelona was the most anarchic place in Europe at the time, and the intellectuals were calling for Catalonian independence. Anarchist literature did the rounds, and Picasso fit right into the anti establishment vibe. Real blood had been shed, and this was far from just being a philosophical rebellion; it was a full on violent revolt. There had been bombings and recent deaths, and the bomber who had caused so much horror at the opera house two years before Picasso's arrival was painted by Barcelona based artists, quite literally, as some kind of martyr. These were turbulent times, and Barcelona was at the complete opposite end of the spectrum of activity to the relatively calm Malaga.

Art wise, Picasso began to do seriously good work as soon as he arrived in Barcelona. Christ Blessing the Devil is an early Picasso gem, but the work harbours a more holy, yet slightly unsettling feel in the following year. As it happens, 1896 was a vital year in his progress and it's odd that this committed atheist chose to paint so much religious imagery. Not only that, but the religious themed material seems to exude a shining holiness, a glow even, that it could not have had if he truly were a pure atheist.

In my view, the two most powerful works in this era are The Altar Boy, aesthetically perfect and astounding when considering he was only fifteen when he painted it, and First Communion, perhaps the moment he proved he could be a monumental artist. Judging by this work, Picasso could easily have gone down the conventional path as his father so wished. No doubt, Jose must have been very proud when gazing at these two foreboding, visually impressive specimens.

Other works however, much less celebrated, make more sense when considering Picasso as the anarchic atheist. To please himself, he drew more personally relevant sketches. Most striking is the oil and charcoal work depicting Jesus with no face. It is, in fact, a very unsettling picture. His hair blowing to one side, the concaved chest, outspread arms and rustic background all give the picture a reserved sense of drama, but the fact Christ is faceless, therefore emotionless, gives the picture its true defiance. The distinct lack of a cross, nails or blood highlights Pablo's lack of inner faith, the crucifixion diminished in an instant. It's as if Pablo was confessing in private that religion held no answers, offered no explanation, and existed for no reason.

Pablo was making good friends in Barcelona, his first close one being fellow artist Manuel Pallares, who he sat beside in class. "He was way ahead of the others," recalled his friend much later. "He paid no attention to what the professors were saying... He could go for hours without saying a word." He was much more animated at their favourite cafe however, The Eden Concert, formerly the Happiness Cafe. His friends there included Ramon Reventos and Angel de Soto, with whom he would roam the streets and visit brothels. It was in one Chinatown based whorehouse where Picasso first lost his virginity. That he gave away his purity via a hired temptress is an essential detail in Picasso's life. The "paid" sex act is one organised and orchestrated by the male, where the female offers unresisting flesh and lives out the fantasies of the patron. It's about control, organising ones' desire to ones' taste. Perhaps it explains much of Picasso's later views towards women, the fact he believed they should do as he pleased, and no doubt solidified his unarguable misogyny.

Away from the brothels, he entered art competitions but failed to win. Faint press notices were all well and good for his reputation, but did little for his proper artistic advancements. In 1897 however, his landmark work Science and Charity was met with acclaim. The startling picture is one of Picasso's early best. The painting presents a dark image; a woman is dying in bed, with a nun on one side offering comfort while holding a little girl, and a doctor seated at the other, assessing the situation and the girl's decreasing health. It was Jose who suggested Picasso work on a larger scale, and when he agreed he paid homage to his father by using him as the model for the doctor.

Very academic, it appears that the structure and lay out was influenced by Jose's teachings (one can imagine him advising young

Pablo from over his shoulder). Indeed, it lacks the individuality of Pablo's more characteristic work to come later, though using that word seems rather ill fitting, considering the breathtaking range Picasso had throughout his life. It could have come from a thousand other artists of the period, but it is no doubt an impressive painting. Deservedly, accolades were poured over him. Pablo received a positive mention at the Madrid Fine Arts Exhibition that year and won the gold medal at Malaga's Provincial Exhibition. It was a huge step up.

The painting itself harbours the compassion and detail in all his best early work, especially in the face of the woman, whose features and air of needy desperation he based on a beggar lady he spotted on the streets of Barcelona. His father was delighted with the feedback, and hilariously one of his friends wanted to "christen" Pablo officially as an artist by pouring a bottle of champagne over his head. The picture and its glowing feedback presented Pablo with a predicament; should he go the avant-garde difficult route and opt for change against all odds, or go for the glory, the big canvases, the world of well paid academia, acceptance and acclaim? He would choose the former, but only after a period of mulling it over.

Pablo and his friend Pallares used to hang around on the roof of his Barcelona studio (paid for by his father), throwing stones at passersby. One day they hit a man on his top hat, which attracted the interest of a passing policeman. In a scenario you just wish there was photographic evidence of, Picasso and his friend hid behind the huge canvas on which was painted Science and Charity while the angry officer banged on the door. Picasso was beginning to rebel more, and though he had admired his father earlier in life, he now almost had to remould him in his mind as a figure to react against. After all, he was a beaten man, a painter who had been chewed up and spat out by the academic establishment. Jose strove for the kind of acceptance that Picasso was establishing himself against. Though it seems unfair given Jose's financial and emotional support, his enthusiasm for his son's work, Picasso now viewed him as a defeated victim of a system that was hopelessly outdated. Casting the stones at the suited man on the street metaphorically represented his need for rebellion, even if he could have easily wound up one of those top hatted gents himself.

There is a certain sadness to these changing views on his father. As an old man himself, Pablo said "Every time I draw a man I think of my father. To me, man is Don Jose, and he will be all my life." Deep inside, he still admired and loved the man, but those cruel portraits of him looking drained, gaunt and sunken were half catharsis and half self preservation. He had to believe his father was part of the machine, a cog in the agonising grind, another enemy who represented rigidity, even if beneath the surface he worshipped the man as a hero.

Still, in this era he was becoming a fine academic painter. The self portrait of himself dressed in eighteenth century garb, painted a year earlier in 1896, could have been complete a hundred years earlier, not just for the fashion trends but the technique and style itself. His Portrait of Aunt Pepa is also a captivating painting, while his other self portraits show a distinct development also. Self Portrait with Short Hair captures Picasso looking more boyish than ever, a face of innocence, staring out at the observer without a shred of consciousness. (Remarkable, really, to think that he was already visiting brothels at this point.) The Self Portrait with the Fringe is even better, with young Pablo harbouring some cockiness - this one must surely have been a more accurate portrait than the others, especially considering his attitude at the School of Fine Arts. He gives himself a graceful classicism, but an attitude in the eyes and features that suggests the setting is only a temporary one.

When he visited Malaga in the summer holidays, he once again turned to the bullfight for artistic inspiration. His 1896 Bullfighting oil painting is wonderful, all haziness and vague shapes suggesting the brutality from a distance, rather than revelling in it as he would in later works. The painting features a sprawled dead creature, perhaps the horse sacrificed for the bull or the defeated bull itself, while the bullfighter stands in the centre of the ring. The crowd, nothing more than blobs of colour, effortlessly embody the enraptured excitement of the bullfighting spectators better than any detailed depiction ever could. His love of the sport is evident.

The other key works of 1896 are his portraits of Jose. One is classy, sepia in tone and sympathetic to the sitter. Jose, in profile, seems full faced, dignified, respectful. Clearly, Picasso has purposely portrayed his father with respect. But later in the year, in a ghostly blue side-portrait, he appears gaunt, dead eyed, rigid and far from graceful. Could this perhaps reflect his diminishing attitude towards his father in that year of 1896? Strangely, the latter work could have fit easily into the Blue Period, still four years away at this point; and not just for the obvious reasons that it contains the colour blue. No, the work harbours a heaviness, a sadness, a weight which is impossible to ignore. Pablo may not have been feeling any great sadness personally, but was perhaps attempting to depict the sense of bitter defeat Jose felt against the art world. Comparing Jose in these two portraits though, it's as if we are looking at two different men; or more essentially, two different viewpoints done months apart, from the eyes of a young man growing increasingly disillusioned with his father. The contrast between the two images effortlessly embodies the inevitable trials of teenage rebellion.

At the end of 1897 having achieved success with Science and Charity, Pablo turned sixteen. Against his wishes, he went off to Madrid to further his art studies at the Royal Academy. He trained under Don Antonio Munoz Degrain who taught Picasso how to paint landscapes. Those landscapes, such as House in a Wheatfield (1898) have often been overlooked in Picasso's oeuvre (though there was a book published in the 1990s all about his landscape work) they show that by the end of the century, and not yet even near twenty, he was mastering all areas of paint, and was developing techniques far beyond his years.

Pablo really was the spoilt teenager. As well as support from his father who remained back in Barcelona with the rest of the family, Uncle Salvador and his two aunts sent money to ensure his life was a little easier in Madrid. He referred to the help as a "mere pittance. Barely enough to keep from starving, no more." He was secretly grateful of course, but as with his views on his father, this attitude was adopted out of a loyalty to his rebellious streak rather than outright resentment. After all, without this "pittance" Pablo would not have been able to survive.

Pablo also detested the so called teachers at the art school, saying in a letter to a friend that year, "They haven't a grain of common sense. They just go on and on about the same old stuff. You can hardly believe the nonsense they talk... Here in Spain it's not that we are as stupid as we've always been made out to be, it's just that we're very badly educated. If I had a son who wanted to be a painter I wouldn't keep him here in Spain for a moment. I don't believe in following any particular school, for all it leads to is mannerism and affectation in the painters who do it." Paradoxically, he also said he would not send this imaginary son to Paris, even though that was the place he himself wished to be. Even at this stage, he knew that Paris was the goal.

Though he hated his lessons, he did enjoy roaming the museums and art galleries, gazing in wonderment at the El Greco and Velazquez masterpieces. Clearly, these were the people he wished to emulate, but little did he know that in his own life time he would surpass them in influence and importance. He also enjoyed the girls Madrid had to offer on the streets and in brothels. He often thought of a girl he had been with in Barcelona, named Rosita, and in his letter to a friend that year he reserved some kisses for her. This mysterious girl was once dubbed a lady of the night, but it is now revealed she was a circus performer - one of John Richardson's many discoveries was an 1897 circus poster she was featured on - perhaps explaining Picasso's interest in the performers and harlequins which so obsessed him in the later Rose period.

After a short while, Picasso grew bored of the Academy and started spending more time with the pretty girls of Madrid. Slacking off terribly, he stayed in bed until after dinner and spent hours in the local park, drawing in sketchbooks as the clock ticked away. He seems to have had no fixed address for any long period of time, moving from one place to the next. It was not a happy or fulfilling time. When his aunts and uncle learned of his loose life style they cut off their steady payments. Clearly, they would only reward Pablo if he worked hard. Still, nothing Pablo did would make his father follow suit, and he always made excuses for his son. Out of loyalty and commitment, he sent across as much money as he could.

That same year Pablo was struck with scarlet fever and returned speedily to Barcelona. He continued to draw and paint, though few works from 1898 stand out as Science and Charity had previously. He seems to have been stuck between styles at this stage and has no true voice of his own. Yes, there are some pleasant works, such as his rose painting (the three yellow roses) and many of the drawings in his sketch books, which reveal portraits of friends and the kind of things which occupied his mind. Still, Picasso seems aimless at this point.

Bored in Barcelona, he took off with his friend Pallares and hopped on a train to the village of Horta de Saint Joan. He stayed for over half the year, working solidly and spending time with friends. It proved to be another vital trip. The structure of the village would later influence his cubist period, and he returned there over a decade later to paint.

"Whatever I know I learned in Horta" he boldly claimed, even though he had said something similar about Barcelona. Still, he seems to have had some kind of spiritual breakthrough in Horta. For a short spell Pablo and his friend spent time at Pallares' family home, but they both wanted to spread their wings. Teaming up with a young gypsy boy, they set out into mountains to find themselves. Like his hermitic uncle before him, Pablo rejoiced in living remotely in a cave, though he did have his two friends for company and he had the comfort of Pallares' young brother visiting them everyday on mule-back with supplies. Pablo slept on a bed of grass and for hours the

61

friends sat around a fire. It was far and away from the comforts of the family home, but Pablo enjoyed the rustic freedom of this new lifestyle.

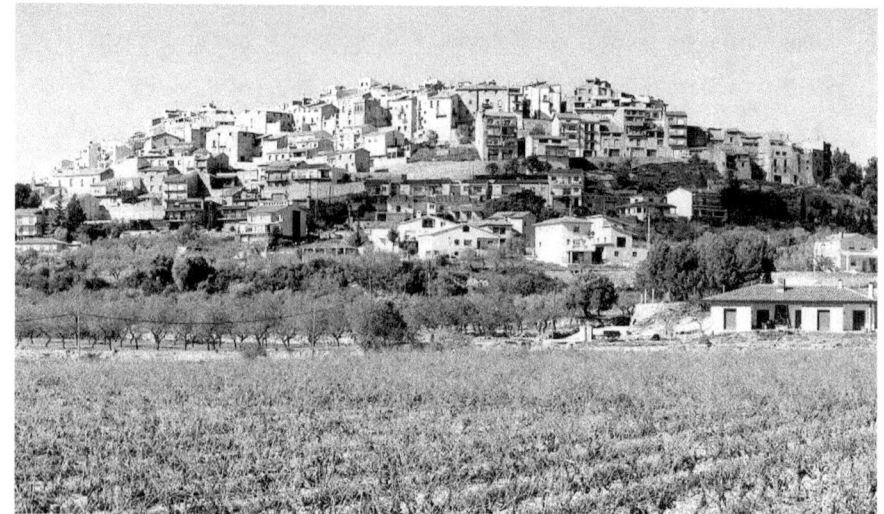

Horta, the village Pablo retreated to when frustrated with Barcelona.

"I like Horta very much. Sometimes I think I should have stayed to live there, but my friends told me: What will you do there? I don't know, I don't know; perhaps I would feel better than now."
- Picasso, 1969

Through the day Picasso, Pallares and the gypsy boy sat painting, learning about colours, blending and the importance of variety. Though the importance of the gypsy differs in both men's respective recollections (Pablo says his presence was vital, while Pallares barely mentions him), this was a time that Pablo looked back upon romantically, as if the gypsy were some great love of his, a muse perhaps. Was the gypsy boy his first muse?

The paradise was cut short when the gypsy fled, stating that he *had* to leave. He said that if he stayed he'd have to kill Pablo, because he was not a true gypsy. Soon after, Pablo went back to Barcelona, disillusioned and deflated. He arrived in February of 1899, entering a dark period in his art, in some ways darker than parts of the later Blue Period. If they had dubbed this era like they would the Blue and Rose, it would certainly be known as the Black Period (often the term used for his African influenced age, though they use the word more literally). This is an awkward period for Pablo and remains so for Picasso studiers. He was openly rebelling against his father and refusing to re-enter the art school in Barcelona, therefore stuck in an artistic limbo. It is important to remember he was not yet even 18 years old, so for a boy of that age he was certainly an accomplished artist. Indeed, it is equally important not to judge his early work in comparison to his later landmark masterpieces, for even his teenage work is more accomplished than most artists' "mature" work.

He was working in Santiago Cardona's small studio in this period, situated above a corset shop. Though no longer studying, Jose refused to criticise his son and wrote to his wife from Madrid that he was glad Pablo was in employment, though he still openly regretted he had done very little of worth the previous year.

It was around this time that Pablo began to hang around the 4 Cats cafe in Barcelona, where fellow artists hung around and discussed art, politics and literature. He met a life long friend there, Jaime Sabartes, a long haired bespectacled Catalonian who immediately connected with Pablo.

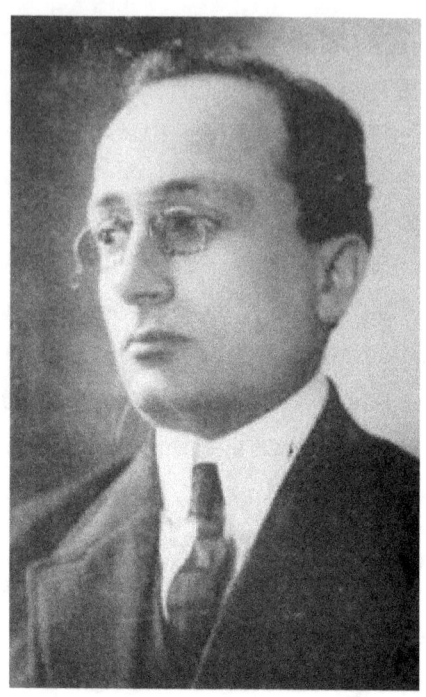

Jaime Sabartes, pictured in 1913.

"We spoke of him as of a legendary hero..."

Sabartes later wrote of his first meeting with Picasso: 'Of my first visit to the studio in the street of Escudellers Blancs I still conserve the memory of the farewell. It was midday. My eyes were still impregnated with what I had seen on his papers and in his note books... Picasso, standing in the corner of the angle formed by the corridor that passed in front of the fourth studio, he rummaged into my confusion with that fixed gaze of his. On passing in front of him to say goodbye I insinuated a sort of reverence, surprised by the magic force revealed to me: the marvellous power of the Magi who offer presents which are so rich in surprises and hopes. "

At this point it's important to remember Pablo was still being referred to as Pablo Ruiz Picasso, using both his mother's maiden name and his father's surname. Sabartes liked the ring of Picasso better and was the first person to repeatedly utter it. Ruiz was more common, Picasso more unusual. In time, Sabartes' preference of the more exotic name would have an effect on Pablo.

Pablo made another key friend in this era that would be important in his life and to his development as an artist in a very different way. He moved into a studio at Riera de San Juan with fellow painter Carles Casagemas. As his father was the consul for the USA in Barcelona, he had little money problems and didn't mind covering the whole rent. Meanwhile, Picasso worked away, throwing away his academic chains and taking on his new life as an artist following his passion. It's often been said that at around 1900 he stopped painting what he saw and began painting what he felt. Though it's easily to over enhance the myth of this era, there is a great feeling that something amazing was about to happen, too amazing for Picasso himself to fully understand.

Before skipping straight to 1900 though, easily the first monumental year in his life, 1899 reveals the roots of that breakthrough time. His portraits have taken on yet more depth, though they are often bleak to the point of feeling suffocating.

There may be more well known and celebrated portraits of Casagemas, albeit ones painted after the fateful incident which changed the course of Picasso's art (more of that later), but I feel the one piece which captures the legendary gloom and mythical doom of

Carles is the 1899 portrait Picasso did of him. Carles is staring straight at the observer, clad in a long brown coat, his deathly eyes haunting and penetrating from beyond the grave. It feels photographic, so intense is the depiction of this doomed young man.

One of the finest works from this year is what appears to be a half finished self portrait. The young Picasso seems to have imagined himself more mature than his seventeen and half years would have permitted, but there is an elegance to the work which cannot be overlooked. The shading behind him, matching his clothes, seems to have been applied hurriedly. It's more of an illustrative work and not a major piece at all, but for me it stands out, as obscure and buried it may be. It was a good year for portraits, either done in Malaga or Barcelona. The Lola portraits are very strong, the two famous ones varying drastically in tone and presentation, illustrating his knack of variety at the time. His picture of Jaime Sabartes, blue and bespectacled, again pre-dates the so called Blue Period by two years (again, highlighting the broadness of Picasso terminology, which tends to overlook the fact that themes and styles came and went through the years randomly) while his portrait of Angel Soto is terribly romantic, hazy and clouded. My personal favourite of that year is the cartoonish drawing of Picasso and Casagemas, looking like two Dickensian characters; hatted and shady with their collars turned up on their coats to face the cold of the city.

It is the duality of these two very different which becomes the predominant image of this era of Picasso's life, and it's hard not to get swept up in the romantic myth of these lean, naive days. The afore mentioned drawing tidily conjures the wonderment of this hopelessly romanticised idea, as does the surviving photo of the two artists clapping along to Angel Soto playing the flute. Looking at the two figures as they were though reveals many differences. Picasso was self assured in his own way, but Casagemas was anything but. In some ways a strange young man, he at this point had an infatuation with his sister's daughter. He was shy, complicated and prone to bouts of depression and severe self doubt. Picasso tried to show Carles the wonders of the brothel, but he rarely if ever got physical with any of the prostitutes. Casagemas preferred to roam the graveyards of Barcelona, revelling in his own sense of gloominess. Fun was not in his vocabulary.

Hanging with more intellectual and well read friends at the 4 Cats, Picasso soaked up their knowledge and learned as much as he could about literature and philosophy. Though he did not attempt to read the books, his friends had, and they were ready and willing to share their learned wisdom. He did have a personal attachment to Nietzsche's The Will to Power, which rung true with his hopes for freedom and liberation. Indeed, Picasso was no fierce intellect, but he was sure that personal freedom held the key for him.

At the start of 1900, as if to bring in the new century in style, he had another exhibition, his first proper one in fact, at 4 Cats. Sabartes claims that they "wanted to pit Picasso against the idol of Barcelona (Casas) and enrage the public."

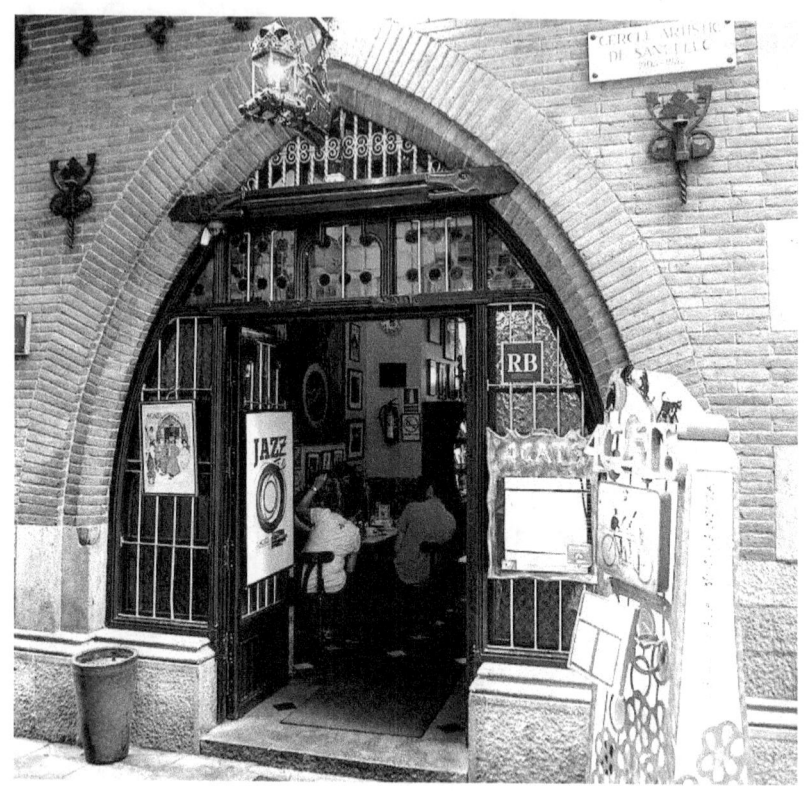

The 4 cats cafe today.

With Pablo elevated to near God status already by his loyal friends, he was more than confident enough to exhibit his portraits for the whole of the city. Some reviews were good, complimenting Picasso's assured style, but one in particular noted Picasso's lack of evenness. "A lack of experience," they continued in La Vanguardia, "Carelessness..." The words stung Picasso more because they were written by an art teacher, Manuel Codoloa. To be put down by the type of man he mocked while studying art only riled Picasso up even more, and now he was keener than ever to fight against the stiff and rigid establishment.

Picasso had made up his mind. There was only one place where his art would be embraced and given the credit it deserved, and that was Paris. He had been reading the art journals lying around at the 4 Cats and was mulling over the decision for some time. His father Jose agreed to give him the train money, so firm he was in the aims and ambitions of his son. In the build up to his visit he did a series of vibrant bullfighting paintings. After his brief death obsession, the series of paintings shown at the 4 Cats in July were like a breath of fresh air and they reflected his new found positivity.

Pallares had planned to head to Paris with Picasso but had prior engagements and stayed behind, catching up with him later on. In the end, Pablo went alone with Casagemas, the two young men clad in tailor made black suits for the occasion. As if bidding farewell to a solider going off to war, his mother and father accompanied Picasso to the train station to wave goodbye. He was Paris bound, and the future was his.

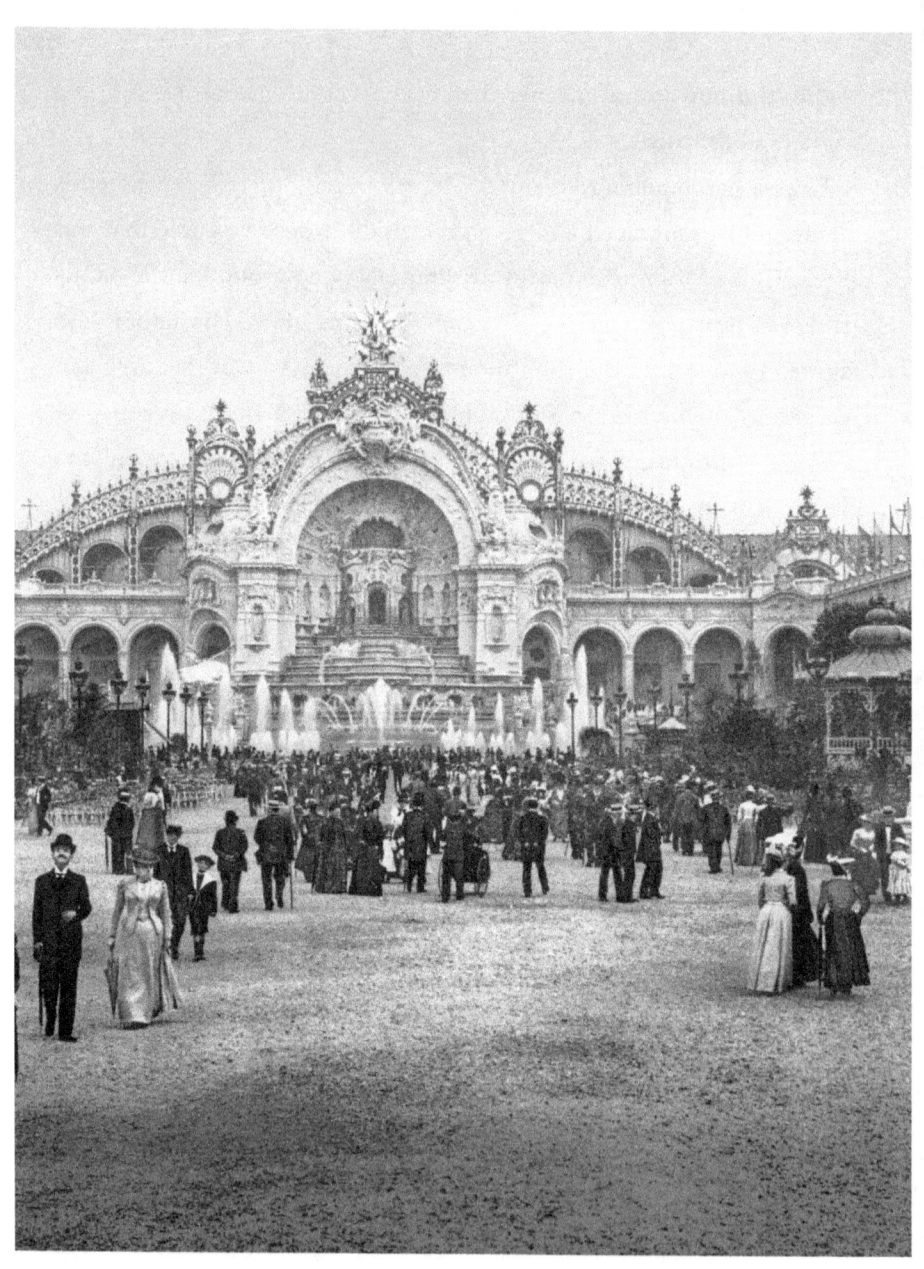

The 1900 Paris World Fair, where young Picasso was heading.

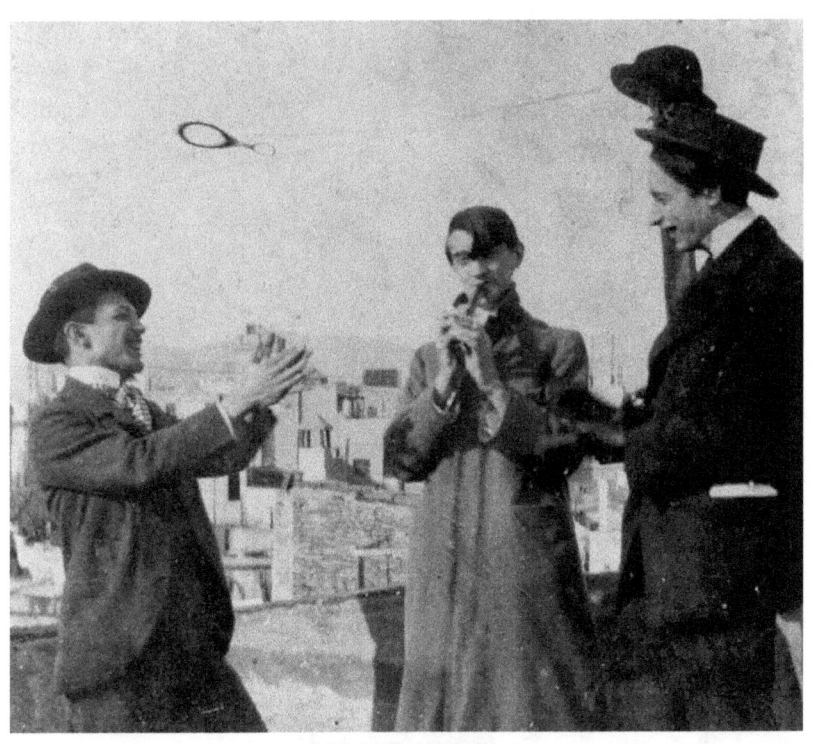

TO PARIS

Art, Love, Gain and Loss

Picasso was not yet nineteen when he arrived in Paris, wide eyed and ready to rise to the very top of the art world. Picasso immediately fell in love with the city, which he and Casagemas explored from corner to corner; the streets, the cafes, the galleries, the night shows and, of course, the brothels. To Picasso, this vibrant and fascinating place was the stuff of dreams. The two young men stayed in a hotel at first and then moved on to a studio. Speaking no French, and mocked whenever trying to do so, he stuck with Catalonians, including Casagemas and Manuel Hugue, the art collector based there in Paris.

He and Casagemas celebrated Pablo's 19th birthday in style, as detailed in Casagemas' colourful letter to his and Pablo's friend Ramon Reventos, illustrated by Picasso in typical style.

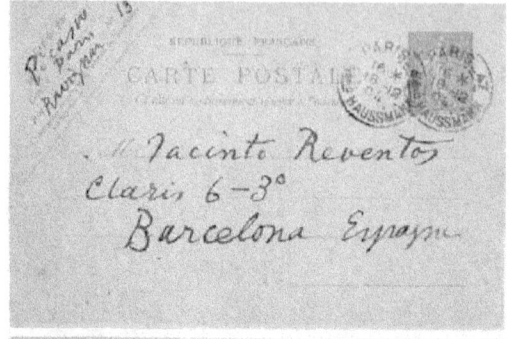

A letter Picasso and Casagemas sent back to Ramon Reventos and family.

Picasso spent much of his time in Paris womanising, and one girl in particular, a model named Odette, seems to have been more treasured than the others. Neither spoke one another's language, though that seemed to matter very little to the testosterone fuelled Picasso, who spoke the language of lust well enough. Casagemas on the other hand, though not engaging in carnal activities, had fallen for a girl by the name of Germaine Gargallo Pichot, "the woman of my thoughts" as he called her. Though he was prone to developing obsessions with certain females from time to time, his love and pining for her seemed different somehow.

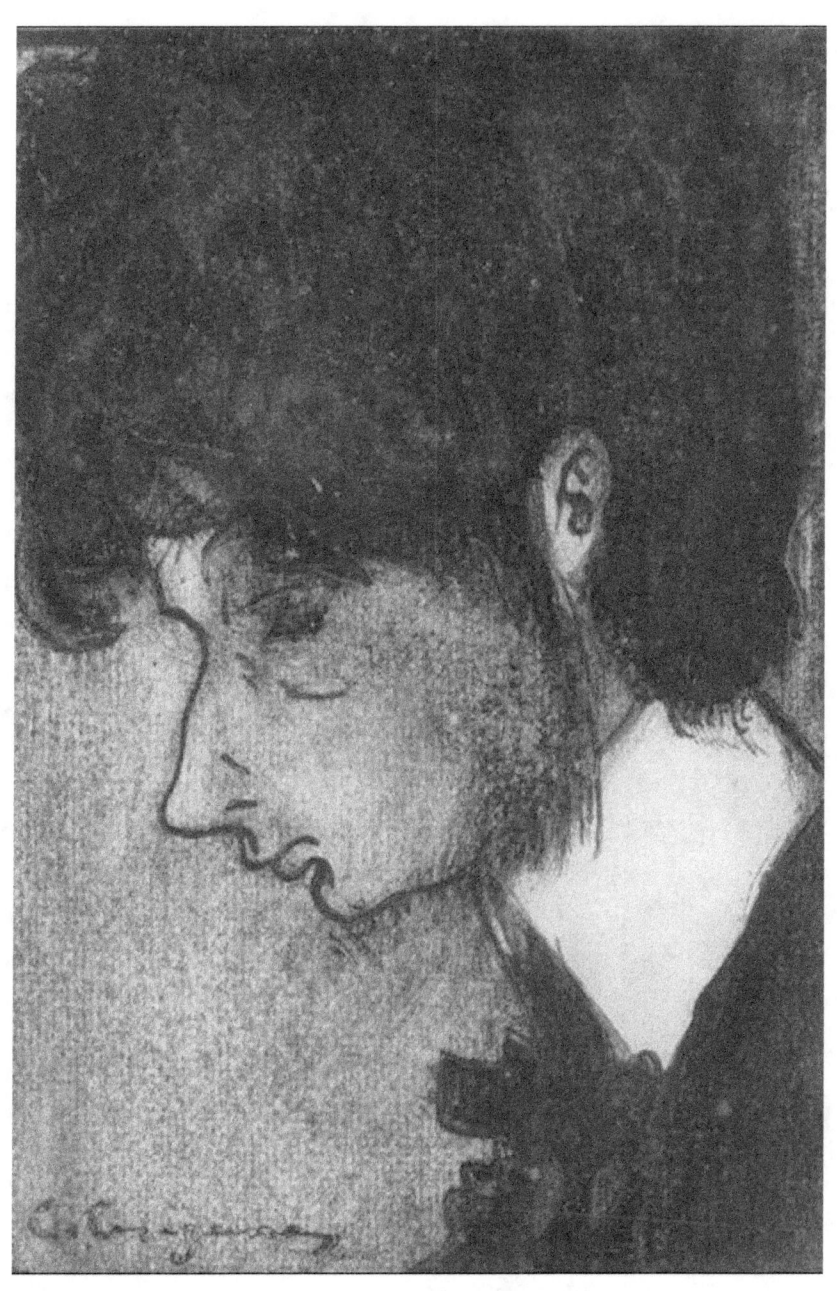

A Casagemas self portrait.

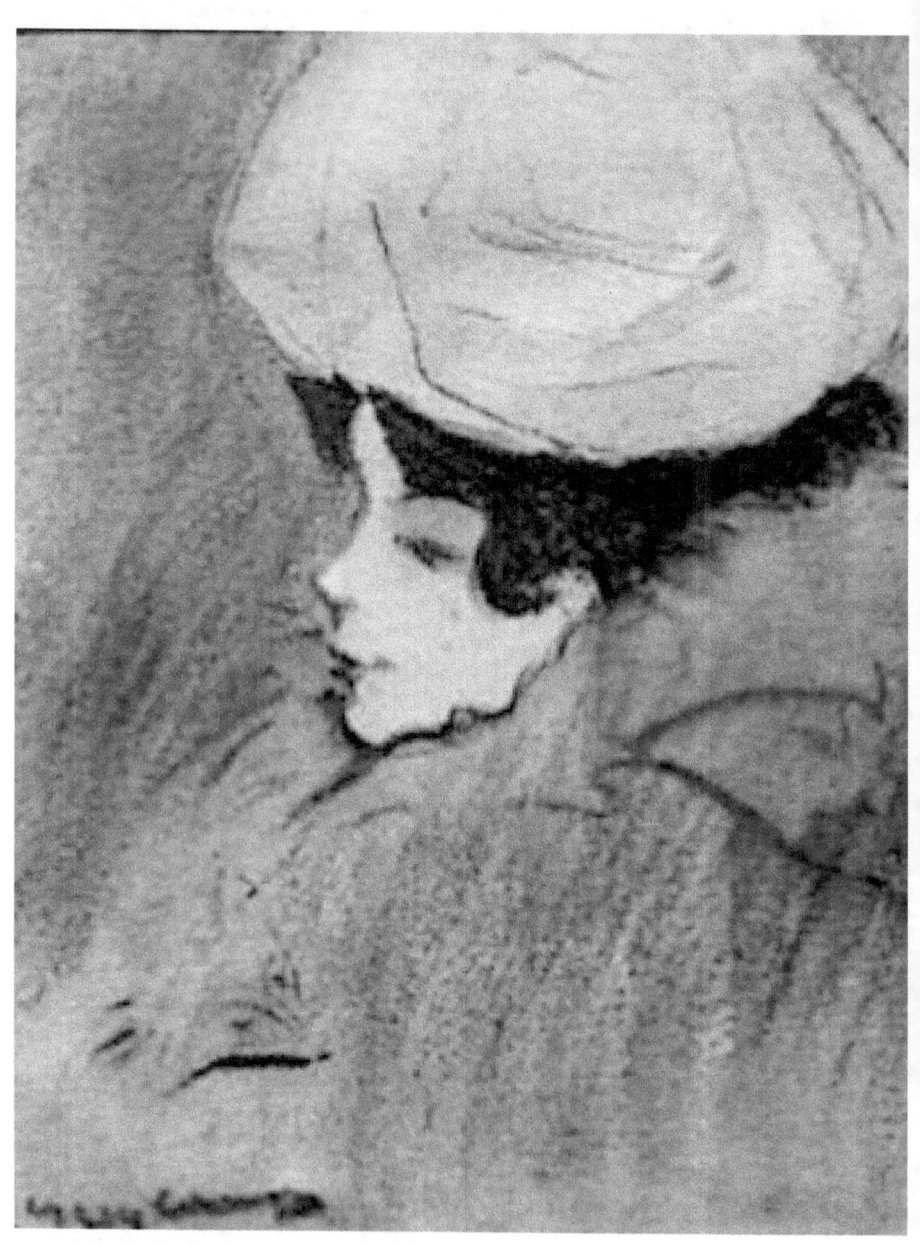

A Casagemas portrait of Germaine.

While Picasso was off living and loving guilt free, Casagemas only had one woman in his sights. If he couldn't have her, the world would end. Picasso was adamant however that though they spent a lot of time "fondling", the women did not interfere with the true goal; the journey to the absolute - their art.

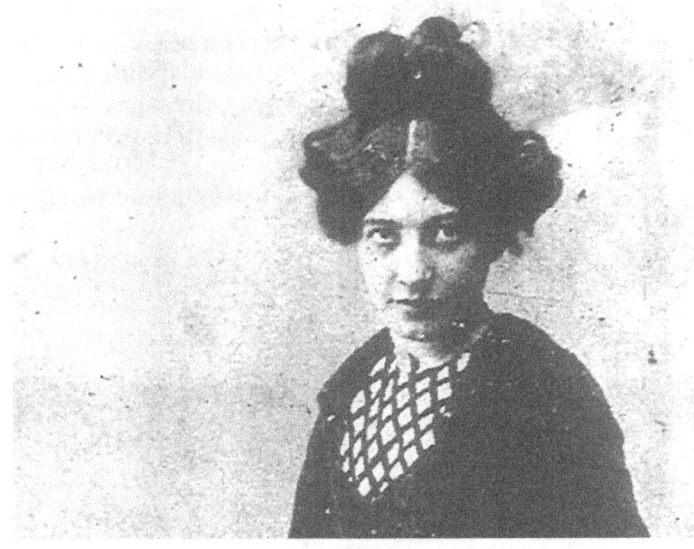

Germaine Gargallo, the object of Casagemas's desires.

While in Paris, Picasso developed a fond love for Toulouse Lautrec, and even sold a painting, Le Moulin de la Galette, that was a clear homage to him. "It was in Paris," he later said, "that I realised what a great painter Lautrec was." When Picasso painted the Moulin Rouge and the cabarets of Parisian night life, he knew he was following in the footsteps of legends like Lautrec and Renoir. That he was not intimidated or put off by their towering reputations tells one a lot about Picasso's confidence in his own work.

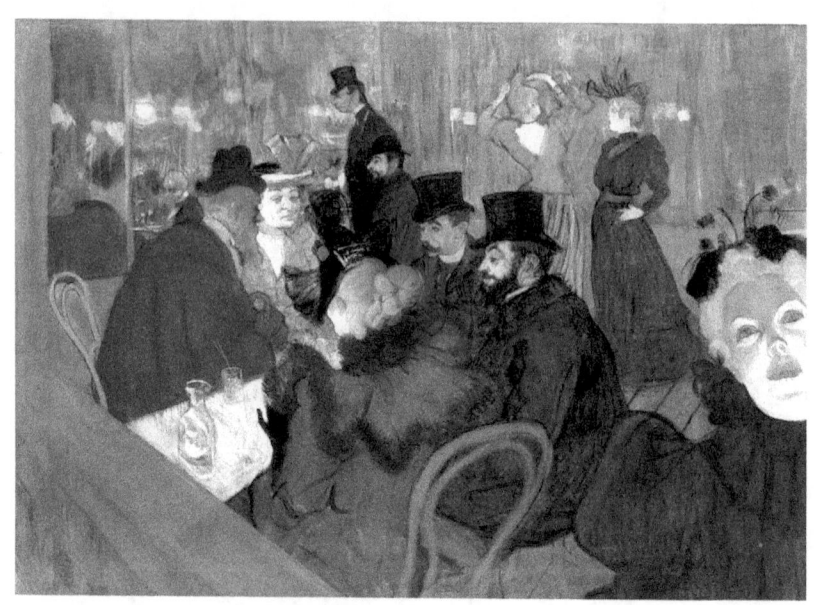

Above: The work of Toulouse Lautrec was a huge inspiration to Picasso while on his first trip to Paris. As was the work of Renoir, pictured below.

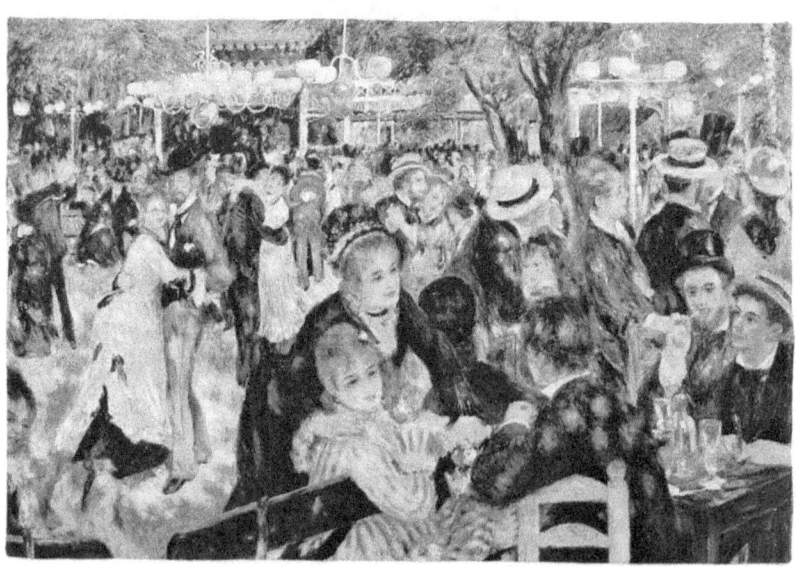

A key figure on his first Paris trip was the art dealer Pere Manyac, a fellow Catalan who met Picasso and was immediately struck by his strength of character. He began paying Picasso 150 francs a month for exclusive ownership of his work. He also introduced Picasso to other areas of the city he was less confident to venture, given his lack of experience there, naivety and poor French skills. He was introduced to other prominent people, like Berthe Weill, a gallery owner who was brought round to Picasso's lodgings to see his work, only to find him unwilling to answer the door. When they eventually entered, they found him in bed with a male friend; it had been a childish prank. Again, it was his rebellious streak coming through. As when he belittled his aunt and uncles' kindness as "a pittance", he was disrespecting a patron for the hell of it.

Within two months, Picasso had left Paris after his first taste of its glories and returned to Barcelona, his home if he truly had one. After a brief stay, he and Casagemas took a trip down to Malaga, but they were turned away from hotels due to their long hair and scruffy appearance. Clearly, hotel owners thought them trouble, for they looked suspiciously like anarchists. In the end, his aunt convinced the Tres Naciones that he could be trusted, and he and Carles checked in.

Picasso was glad to be back home in Malaga, but Casagemas was depressed, pining for Germaine, the woman he longed for but had shunned him coldly. Picasso tried to cheer him up with revelry but to no avail. In the end, Casagemas grew tired of his friend's jollity and eventually returned to Paris once more, evidently to win the heart of his beloved. Picasso went to Madrid to give his art career a go in the capital. He ended up starting an art magazine with the writer Francesc d'Assis Soler, called Arte Joven, translated in English to

Young Art. The aim of the publication was to start a new world order, wipe the slate clean and begin a revolution of sorts. It wound up being far from revolutionary of course, but was a nice distraction for a Picasso in limbo.

While he was working on the first issue however, he received a letter delivering crushing, utterly devastating news. Casagemas, his wonderful friend, had shot himself dead in Paris. On the 17th of February 1901, he had visited Germaine and a few other friends at Montmartre's Hippodrome cafe, pulled out a gun and attempted to kill the woman he loved so dearly. When the bullet missed her, he turned the gun on himself, and uttered the immortal words, "So much for me.."

Casagemas' mother was so destroyed that she died of shock on the spot upon receiving the horrible news. The effect of the death on Pablo was not overtly noticeable, nor was it instantaneous, but it would grow in complexity and depth over the following months. He felt numerous emotions in one, mostly guilt about having let him go back to Paris alone. Surely, had he gone with him Pablo could have stopped Carles performing the ritualistic act. Further guilt was brought on by the fact that when Picasso did go back to Paris in May of 1901, he started an affair with Germaine herself, the very woman Casagemas had been unable to satisfy. Worse still, in time Picasso moved into the lodgings Casagemas had already paid for, sharing the bed with Germaine. It was a betrayal of sorts, but also symbolic. If Casagemas couldn't make it happen with Germaine, then Pablo surely could, meaning in a very bizarre and twisted way that his sacrifice had not been in vein.

À mes chers amis
Suzanne et Henri
Picasso
1904

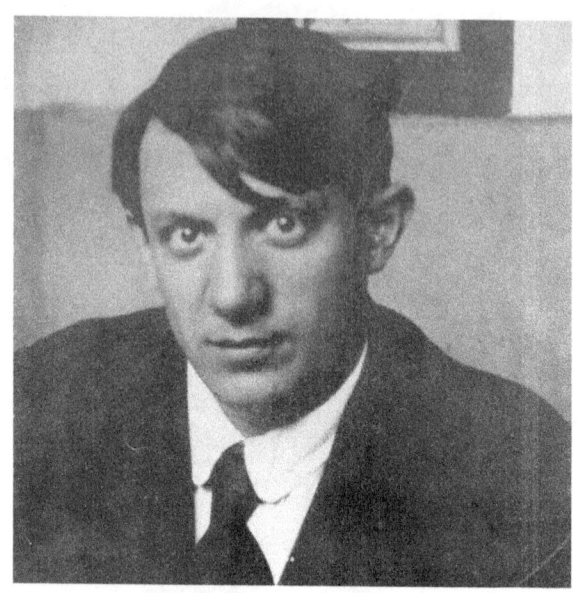

DAYS OF BLUE AND ROSE

An Artist in Transition

The periods this book covers are what I truly feel to be the formative years of Pablo Picasso's artistic development. The death of Casagemas, often sidelined to justify the sudden arrival of the Blue Period (clearly inspired by the suicide, as Picasso himself claimed it was), is perhaps more important in his story than some people might imagine.

The pair had had an argument before they departed company, over what however it is unknown. At a Casagemas exhibition in Barcelona in 2014, Eduard Valles had some ideas about Picasso and Casagemas, and their final chapter as friends: "The theory I put forward, based on new information, contends that instead of going to Paris, as he had anticipated, Casagemas travelled from Barcelona to Madrid to meet up with Picasso... But given Picasso's character, the latter would have utterly cold-shouldered him and Casagemas would have continued on his way to Paris. This hypothesis is supported by dates: between January 28, when he wrote the letter, and February 17, when he committed suicide, there was sufficient time for him to undertake this journey."

The huge crushing guilt he felt at having let down his comrade, his troubled right hand man, led to a commercially unsuccessful phase, much like his earlier, less spoken-of Black Period. But it was not immediate. In May of 1901 he moved into a studio with the art agent Pere Manach, previously belonging to Casagemas, which makes this chapter all the more disturbing for Picasso and the retrospective onlooker. He worked for six weeks to build up enough work for his exhibition for Ambroise Vollard, which eventually ran from the 25th of June until the 14th of July. Today we are unaware of all the works which made the Vollard exhibition, but we do know how popular it was. There is also a photo of Picasso with Manach and Torres Fuster from the period which features some art behind the three men which must have been at the exhibition. Dwarf Dancer and At the Moulin Rouge were some of the key works, but it could be argued that Picasso was merely doing variations on repeated styles and subjects, given he had so little time to gather enough work to fill the gallery. Still, it did very well, and he felt he had made a vast leap as an artist.

"Pablo Ruiz Picasso," wrote the art critic Gustav Coquiot, "an artist who paints all round the clock, who never believes the day is over, in a city that offers a different spectacle every minute. A passionate, restless observer, he exults, like a mad but subtle jeweller, in bringing out his most sumptuous yellows, magnificent greens and glowing rubies".

However, in the second half of the year (though some say the Blue Period began earlier in the year during his time in Malaga after hearing the news of Casagemas) his work took on a more downbeat mood. The buyers he had built up in his first 1901 Ambroise Vollard exhibition, not to mention the critics who had so admired his restlessness, were all but put off by the grimness of the Blue Period. Now, this era is largely celebrated, though it wasn't exactly the tidy time frame it appears to be now in Picasso studies. (Indeed, not all of this era was "blue" either, but there is a gloom hanging over most of these works.) It unfolded organically. But Picasso was definitely a man who painted what he felt, especially when he didn't know exactly what he was feeling. Clearly the death of his friend and the subsequent affair with Germaine had an effect on him. But as Picasso was so driven, self assured and passionate, it was hard for him to channel and get to grips on what he was feeling. Undoubtedly this mixed bag of emotions came out in his work.

"Picasso metaphorically allows his subjects to escape their fate and occupy a utopian state of grace. Some are afflicted with blindness, a physical condition that symbolically suggests the presence of spiritual inner vision."
- National Gallery of Art, 2014

A look at the work in this era though shows the retrospective viewer that Picasso has arrived as a serious expressionist. The whole of 1901 reflects this of course, beginning with the colourful vibrancy of the works at the Vollard exhibition; but it was with the Blue Period that the true artist emerges, for he knows the work is not commercial. It is from the heart, and he *needs* to get it out on the canvas, regardless of whether anyone wants to buy it or not.

"It was thinking about Casagemas that got me started in painting blue," Picasso told Pierre Daix in 1976. He may have been self myth making, but we have to belief the man himself over critics and students of Picasso. He was very poor at the time, but some wonder if he painted the Blue pictures because he was poor, or he was poor because he painted the Blue pictures. Either way, his financial situation was dire at this point.

You only have to glance again at the works to remind yourself how powerful and iconic they have become. They may not have been thought of much at the time, but now they look like blue prints for what followed in the art scene. Yes, they bare hallmarks of older masters such as Edward Munch, but while these pictures capture the souls of their subjects (or targets), they also reveal the soul of Picasso himself, the bullish alpha male, full of sadness, pain and regret.

His Blue Period self portrait remains one of his most startling pieces of work, rarely rivalled in his own gallery of self reflections. He is gaunt, sunken cheeked, unshaven, hungry and moody. He looks, eerily enough, like his father, or how Pablo had depicted the man only half a decade or so earlier. Defeated or wallowing in self pity? It's hard to say, but there is a perverse delight in reliving the grimness of this portrait over and over again, as Pablo stares out from the canvas, dead eyed but not fully hopeless as many of the other lost souls are in this three year period.

Picasso made new vital friends in this period, like the poet Max Jacob, who began to show him new parts of Paris. Still, he mourned old friends in his art. One of his most terrifying and haunting paintings from the Blue Period dealt directly with his fallen comrade. The Death of Casagemas depicts Carles dead in his coffin, from the side, the bullet hole visible in his head and a candle burning brightly. The picture, with its red background, flickering rays of broad colour and the pale green face brings to mind the work of Van Gogh, but it is clear this work has come from within. Pablo may not have been visibly affected by the incident, but it was clearly working on his conscience. He was haunted by the ghost of his departed friend.

Outside his muddled feelings for Casagemas, the Blue Period presents us with destitute figures, as in Mother and Child, and as Picasso enters his twenties and goes into 1902, the blueness seems to have enveloped everything. The Visit (Two Sisters) is among the gloomiest, along with the heavy portrait of the tired and drunk woman. There may be moments of light in this phase (the cabaret painting and the portrait of Angel de Soto with his girlfriend), but the overriding mood is grim; Head of a Dead Woman sums 1902 up the best.

In 1903 though, Picasso's Blue Period hits its peak. The Old Guitarist, perhaps the most famous painting from this era, is staggering to this day, and its effect is down to the details; the crooked spine, aged face, ghostly aura and bony legs. It remains one of his true masterpieces. The Tragedy is another dark but perversely engaging masterwork, the family clad in blue on the gloomy beach exuding sombre defeat. Perhaps the finest of the year, and the one which proves that Casagemas really was floating above the Blue

Period, is the disturbing La Vie, which depicts a nude Germaine hanging on to a dark eyed Carles, as the pair, once again shrouded in foreboding, suffocating blue, gaze at a woman holding a newborn baby. Though x-rays have revealed that this work started as a self portrait, it is important that it ended up as a statement about Casagmeas, his inability to please Germaine, and her subsequent decision to ditch him. The way Carles raises his finger, like the phallus he was unable to control, symbolises his sexual frustration, while there is nothing crueller than making the deceased young man gaze at motherhood and the miracle of birth, the latter achieved one way and one way only, via an act he was unable to perform. It's one of the weightiest and most doom-laden works of the Blue Period.

As 1903 turned to 1904, Picasso's work began to shift and more variants of colour came to the palette, though admittedly there were more colours other than the sombre blue in the Blue Period. Blindness seems to have become a key theme, whether represented literally or used metaphorically; either way, 1904's Selestina (the portrait of the blind beggar), The Frugal Repast and The Blindman's Meal (the latter from the previous year) prove his preoccupation with visual impairment.

1905 is widely regarded as another key year, perhaps the most rounded and proficient of his artistic life so far. Pablo was now living permanently in Paris and his mood was brightening. The dark mood is fading, the clouds are lifting and the subject matter is lighter. Picasso becomes interested in harlequins, acrobats and performers, and his best works from this period all hover in this area. The Rose Period is like a breath of fresh air after the glumness of the Blue years, yet there is still a melancholic air about much of these works, especially The Family of Saltimbanques, Le Lapin Agile (with Picasso in harlequin costume), Boy with a Pipe, Tumblers, Juggler and Boy with a Dog. Still, the paintings are full of variety and a sense of liberation. From here on, Picasso displayed utter confidence and unity as an artist. His popularity grew, the burden of the Blue years was behind him, and nothing but success and artistic freedom awaiting him.

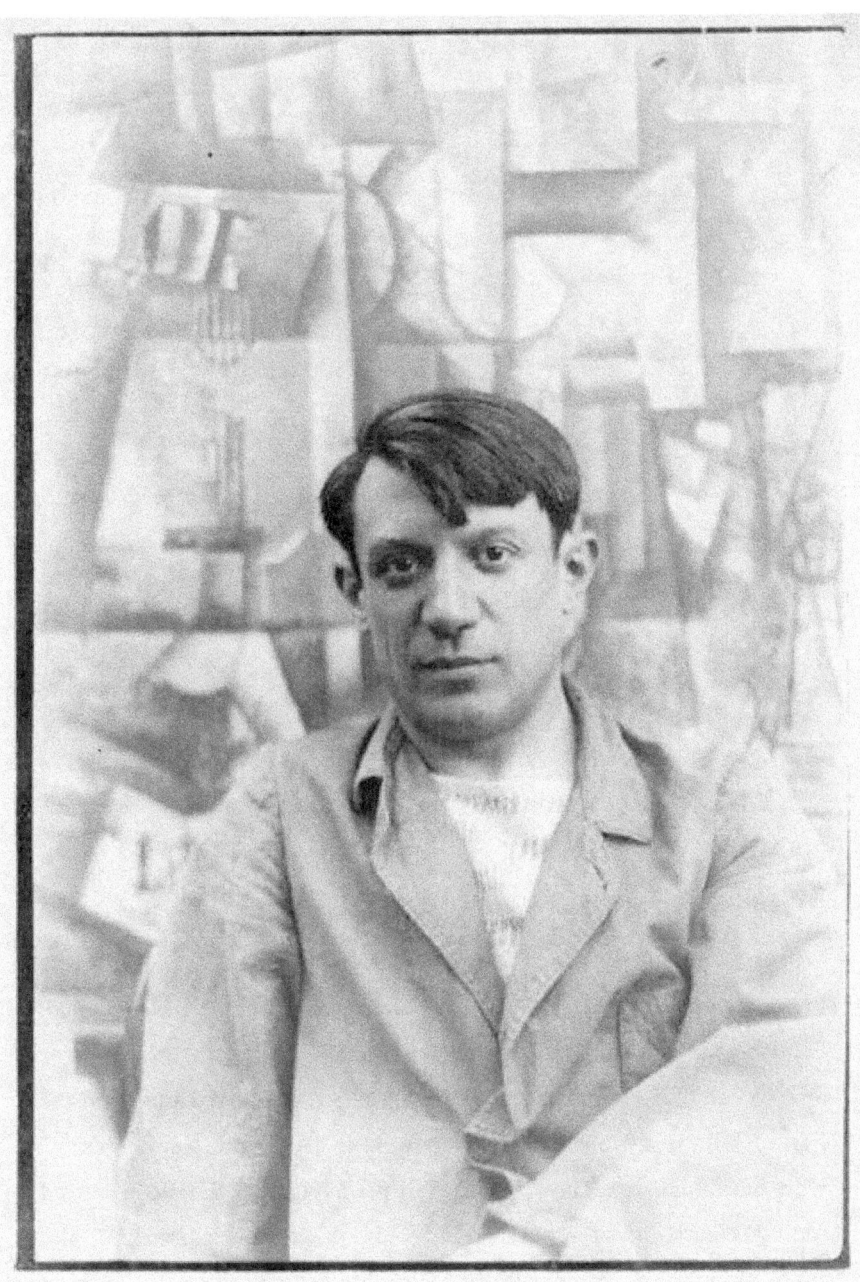

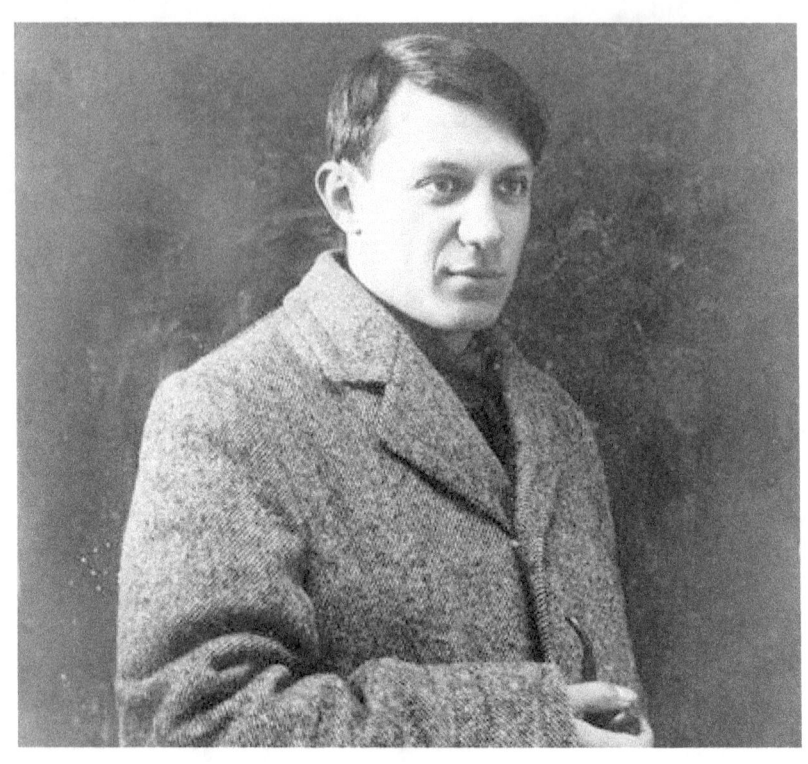

POSTSCRIPT

And the Rest is History

While in the midst of what we now know as the Rose Period, this one being a particularly broad term for the years running 1904 to 1906, Picasso gained a fan and patron in Gertrude Stein, the art collector and writer, and her brother Leo. They began to collect and promote his work, introducing him to key people in Paris, like Henri Matisse, who became a rival and friend. Within a year of the Rose Period fading, Picasso had re-written the rule book with his astonishing and revolutionary Les Demoiselles d'Avignon, his outrageous depiction of the ladies of the Carrer d'Avinyo whorehouse in Barcelona. The work famously led him into cubism and his experiments with Georges Braque, and eventually towards his days of neo-classicalism in the 1920s, when Pablo lived a glamorous and more upmarket life with his wife Olga Khokhlova. From then on, Picasso was not just an artist; in many ways, he *was* art, the most famous painter in the world who everyone, even non art lovers, had at least some awareness of.

The years explored in this book may pale in comparison to what came after - the war years for instance, when he created Guernica - but without them Picasso would not have become the true artist he did. If not for his father, there would have been no art in his life; without Malaga, there would have been no bullfight; no Casagemas, no Blue Period, therefore no artistic freedom and shift into personal expressionism. These years often get overlooked, mainly because there are far fewer "iconic" works within them. But there are just as many important works, ones which not only helped Picasso himself develop and evolve, but the art world as a whole. It was onwards and upwards from here, but in many ways the days of Malaga, A Coruna, Barcelona, Madrid, Horta and the early Parisian era would never leave him.

REFERENCES AND ACKNOWLEDGEMENTS

Some photos in this book were taken by the author in Malaga and Barcelona. All pictures of Picasso himself, along with other location shots, are in the public domain, while some small reproductions were used under fair use to accompany the text.

Books;

Becoming Picasso: Paris 1901, Coultard Gallery

Picasso, Taschen

Picasso: The Blue and Rose Periods

Picasso: The Early Years, Josep Palau i Fabre

Picasso: Early Years, 1892 - 1906, by Marilyn McCully

A Life of Picasso, The Early Years, by John Richardson

Picasso, by Norman Mailer

ABOUT CHRIS WADE

Chris Wade is a UK based writer, filmmaker and musician. As well as running the acclaimed music project Dodson and Fogg, he has written books on The Kinks, Malcolm McDowell, Captain Beefheart, Robert De Niro and many others. He has also released audiobooks of his comedic fiction, such as Cutey and the Sofaguard, narrated by Rik Mayall. His other projects include Rainsmoke, a musical outfit with actor Nigel Planer, and Hound Dawg Magazine, for which he has interviewed such people as Sharon Stone, Donovan and Jethro Tull's Ian Anderson. His art films include The Apple Picker (accepted by Sydney World Film Festival, featuring Toyah Willcox and Nigel Planer), and he also made a documentary on jazz singing Surrealist George Melly.

More info at his website: wisdomtwinsbooks.weebly.com